THE BULL & THE BARRIERS
THE WRECKS OF SCAPA FLOW

THE BULL & THE BARRIERS
THE WRECKS OF SCAPA FLOW

Lawson Wood

TEMPUS

First published 2000
Reprinted 2002, 2004

Tempus Publishing Limited
The Mill, Brimscombe Port,
Stroud, Gloucestershire, GL5 2QG
www.tempus-publishing.com

British Library Cataloguing in Publication Data.
A catalogue record for this book is available from the British Library.

ISBN 0 7524 1753 3

Typesetting and origination by Tempus Publishing Limited.
Printed in Great Britain.

Contents

Acknowledgements

I have been supported by many of the Orkney dive specialists and their boats, but would like to give special mention to Zoe and Andy Cuthbertson and (the) Jean Elaine, professional and helpful, they have helped me on many occasions; Steve Mowat and the Triton; Terry Todd and the Girl Minah; Leigh and Dougie at the Diving Cellar in Stromness; The Northern Diving Group and the Ministry of Defence; Claudia and Carsten Werner for much needed German translations; Der Submarin Archiv, Wilhelmshaven; The Lyness Visitor Centre; Lewis Munro, Curator of the Museum; Kirkwall Library; Lt Cdr Ian Fraser; Reg Rea; RN Submarine Archive; Wright & Logan; Imperial War Museum; National Maritime Museum; British Newspaper Library; Cdr I.G.Milne; National Maritime Museum; Faslane Naval Base; Royal Navy; Orkney Islands Council; Caledonian Macbrayne; Scottish Tourist Board; Lesley Orson; The Ferry Inn; Eleanor at Plainstones.

Foreword

Other than my family, my two great loves in this life are photography while sub aqua diving and local (Scottish) history. I am very fortunate in being able to combine both of these passions, not only as a hobby, but as my profession. I first dived Scapa Flow many years ago and like so many others, was caught up in the intrigue and drama which unfolded around these cold, northern waters. Returning year after year, little by little, the various wrecks revealed more of their secrets to me. Not interested in penetrating these disintegrating hulks in the search for more tangible souvenirs, I was more than content to portray the ships themselves and the marine life which lives on and around them.

I am not the first person to think that the Orkney Islands are magical. Witness the standing stones and stone rings dotted all over the islands and you soon begin to realize that the area is rather special. Scapa Flow itself is the largest, sheltered natural harbour in Europe and it is here that the Home Fleet made its Atlantic base. A prime target for aerial or naval attack, a system of defences was installed to attempt to counter any enemy aggression. These were in the form of anti-aircraft gun emplacements, submarine netting, vigilant patrols and the now famous blockships. It is also here that one of the largest concentrations of shipwrecks in the world is found, the scuttled German High Seas Fleet, dating from 1919.

Although most diving is based on the sunken German fleet, in general terms the blockships are photographically more interesting, primarily because the water is so much clearer at the entrance to Burra Sound. The central location of the German Fleet in Scapa Flow results in little water movement, which is fine for scuba diving but unfortunately tends to trap particulate matter in the water column, resulting in fairly poor underwater visibility. Sadly, this reduces the awe of these massive ships, as you can only see small sections at a time and it takes many dives to suitably explore each shipwreck safely. However, there are several other shipwrecks and remains of the already salvaged fleet, such as gun batteries, so the diving does not need to be restricted to the High Seas Fleet ships. There is also the wreckage of a Second World War German ship, the *F2* and a salvage barge nearby at Lyness, as well as older ships such as HMS *Roedean*.

Whatever your preferences are for diving, the mystique and historical importance surrounding the German High Seas Fleet is undeniable. The wrecks are much more than a sub aqua diver's dream, they are an important part of the Orkneys' naval heritage, having played such a significant part in its history. These ships are thankfully protected now, their watery grave no longer such a mystery to us, yet it is deep enough to deter the more foolhardy persons who may feel that diving on these ancient war horses is not too serious. The ships themselves are disintegrating at an alarming rate, bad visibility and wreckage can result in getting snagged if you are not careful and the depth limitations are such that many divers each year succumb to decompression sickness, or the bends as it is often referred to. This comes from staying too deep, too long and not taking enough time to return to safety at the surface. The diving on the ships is perhaps some of the most advanced in Europe and only those persons properly trained should attempt to dive the German Fleet.

Introduction

Sitting in the early morning calm, the cold air of daybreak was leaving a slight foggy residue around the dive boat, we could see no land, or any other living thing, except a tiny orange marker buoy with some frayed line attached. The natural harbour of Scapa Flow in the Orkney Islands has the largest concentration of shipwrecks in the world and we were about to dive on one of those ancient war-horses, in both eerie and spectacular fashion, dropping through 30m (100ft) of water to arrive near the bows of the *Brummer* in a bay set amidst some of the most dramatic scenery in Europe, considerably heightening the diving experience.

The *Brummer* is just one of the four remaining German light cruisers and three battleships which were scuttled under the orders of Admiral Ludwig von Reuter in 1919. Virtually all of the others sunk at the same time were thoroughly salvaged, but largish bits are still scattered over the seabed.

Through the descending gloom, the graceful arch of the sharp bows approach us and we drop to the stony seabed to gaze upwards in awe at this massive ship lying on her starboard side. The hull is completely festooned in plumose anemones (*Metridium senile*) and feather starfish (*Antedon bifida*). From here we swam along the now vertical decking, past the forward 5.9in gun and approached the superstructure which is mostly collapsed. The central section of the ship is now completely destroyed, blasted apart by salvage divers, however, the stern is mainly intact and the other 5.9in gun can be found. Maximum depth is 36m (120ft) and all too soon it is time to make our way back up the mooring buoy line to safety and the comfort of a warm cabin on board the support dive boat.

Very nice indeed, but not exactly spectacular and certainly not as interesting as many divers say it is. The visibility was poor, there was hardly any light and, due to the extreme depth, I had finished my dive before I had shot all of my film!

There must be more to these shipwrecks, now considered to be one of the few sources of metal not affected by radiation. I could not quite come to terms with diving on massive rusting hulks at the limits of safe air diving exploration, when all I could see was something that resembled a rounded seabed, complete with much more interesting different species of marine life which I could photograph elsewhere in much safer, shallower water with more light and time to enjoy myself.

Scapa Flow is undoubtedly the best wreck diving in Europe and certainly ranks in the top five in the world. There is more wreckage in Scapa Flow than any other location on the planet, certainly enough to keep the scrap-happy more macho side of divers interested for many a dive (and yes that does include several ladies that I know of, who love the place). This deep, formidable, cold, natural harbour has served the warring nations' fleets for centuries. At present there are three German battleships, four light cruisers, a Second World War destroyer (*F2*), two submarines, twenty-seven large sections of remains and salvors' equipment, sixteen known British wrecks, thirty-two block ships and two battleships (the *Vanguard* and the *Royal Oak*), with a further fifty-four sections of wreckage, as yet unidentified.

Considered by many to be impregnable from attack, the bay of Scapa Flow, covering some 190sq.km (120 square miles), is completely sheltered by a ring of protective islands. Situated 25km (15 miles) north of the Scottish mainland, access is by the daily car ferry from Scrabster or by regular flight to Kirkwall airport from Edinburgh and Aberdeen.

There is always a sense of mounting excitement as you approach the Orkney Islands by ferry. The initial huge land mass that looms up out of the early morning mist is the Island of Hoy and as they approach the first of several entrances to Scapa Flow, visitors can see the early signs of the derelict, rusting hulks. The 8,900-ton *Inverlane* spans Burra Sound and once looked like the classic shipwreck from the symbols on admiralty charts, with her prow and forward masts clear of the water and the aft lost to view, the promise of dives to come. Now the ship has collapsed in on itself and has rolled over under the relentless battering from the currents which sweep through Burra Sound four times a day. In Stromness, we disembark next to the harbour where the majority of Scapa Flow's fleet of diving boats is based. Most are converted fishing trawlers, their very experienced skippers and crew eagerly awaiting our arrival.

So what is it that brings the droves of divers from all over the world to an area which is not exactly known for its sun-kissed beaches, crystal clear water and palm trees? In fact I seem to remember the famed Scot's comedian Billy Connolly complaining that he could not take his dog out to relieve itself because he couldn't find any trees! They are interested in a fleet of warships sunk deliberately or otherwise during the last two world wars and principally to dive on the German High Seas Battle Fleet, scuttled in 1919. I have seen many a sewn logo testifying to their derring-do, emblazoned on divers' sweatshirts, 'T' shirts, caps and probably matching socks and pants!

Conditions vary tremendously during the season. Visibility is generally poor and dark on the seabed in the centre of Scapa Flow. Lights should always be used and work-up dives should be undertaken before you do the deeper battleships. Which is why so many of us photographers prefer the blockships at the entrance to Burra Sound, where the average depth is half that of the German warships, which means that there is much more light, more interesting marine growth and it is in much clearer water, as the tidal race at Burra Sound sweeps all sedimentation particles away. However, this also means that you have only limited time on these wrecks and then only at slack tide.

1

The Great Harbour

Scapa Flow was the United Kingdom's main base for the Royal Navy during the two world wars due to its strategic geographical location off the north of Scotland, linking both the North Sea and the Atlantic Ocean. Playing a pivotal role in the control of access to the Atlantic against Germany's naval and merchant fleets, the Grand Fleet was positioned in Orkney for the First World War. Similarly the base was used by the Home Fleet from 1939 to 1945 to contain Hitler's Navy. Scapa Bay was also the rendezvous point for merchant ships *en route* to the Baltic during the Napoleonic Wars from 1789 to 1815.

Graeme Spence, Maritime Surveyor to the Admiralty said in 1812:

> ...the art of Man, aided by all the Dykes, Sea Walls or Break-Waters that could possibly be built could not have contained a better Road stead than the peculiar situation and extent of the South Isles of Orkney have made Scapa Flow... from whatever point the Wind blows, a Vessel in Scapa Flow may make a fair wind of it out to free sea... a property which no other Road stead I know of possesses, and without waiting for Tide on which account it may be called the Key to both Oceans.

These seamen were certainly not the first to recognize the significance of the natural protection offered by Scapa Flow. The name Scapa is derived from the ancient Norse word *skalpr* meaning 'sword scabbard' or *skalpei* which means 'ship' or 'isthmus'. In other words, this area in the Orkney islands was ideal for longships to be protected and beached for repairs. The word Flow comes from *floi* or *fljot* meaning a 'large amount of water', like a fjord.

When you travel around Orkney you cannot help but notice the standing stones and ancient stone rings which predate the Norsemen. They can be traced as far back as the Stone Age, and were used in the Bronze and Iron Ages, as well as by the Picts. Very little is known of these early times, other than the

An early photograph of Scapa Flow showing the Home and Atlantic Fleets, based together at Orkney on 17 April 1900. They were there to attend a review by the Admiral of the Fleet and Prince Albert.

TORPEDO FLOTILLA.
PART OF FLEET OF 27 VESSELS IN SCAPA FLOW AUG 1908.

A slightly later view of Scapa Flow, this time taken in 1908 and now home to the Torpedo Flotilla. Note the small sailing vessel manoeuvring its way between these massive ships at anchor.

Home to the northern herring fleet, Stromness had a very busy harbour filled to capacity with steam drifters. The view has changed very little, but sadly the herring industry has gone. Now the more modern fishing vessels reap another type of harvest from the sea, that of scuba diving tourists to visit the sunken German Fleet and the blockships.

monuments themselves and a detailed history of the Norse occupation was not committed to paper until the thirteenth century in Iceland. The *Orkneyinga Saga* tells the tale of the Earls of Orkney and the occupation of the islands.

Skalpei Floi is still a centre for shipping and commerce, with a massive oil terminal on the Island of Flotta. Scapa Flow has risen to become one of the top scuba diving destinations in the world with world class wrecks dating from the world's last great conflicts.

Scapa Defences

When war broke out in 1914, Admiral Sir John Jellico took over command of the Grand Fleet from Admiral Sir George Callaghan and was disgusted by the poor state of defence on the island for Britain's Navy. From their base headquarters near Scapa Pier, he had over 100 naval ships at his command when war was declared on 4 August 1914. When the *U-18* entered Scapa Flow on 23 November 1914, commanded by Kapitan Leutnant von Hennig, real consternation arose. Fortunately, the U-boat had been rammed by the trawler *Dorothy Grey* and it later beached on the Pentland Skerries. Jellico quickly moved the base to Longhope, which offered much better shelter for the ships

Many people just think of Scapa Flow as the base of Home and Atlantic Fleets, yet Wide Firth to the north of Kirkwall is a splendid, sheltered bay, protected by the islands of Stronsay and Shapinsay to the north and north-east and the bulk of Mainland to the west. This postcard from the turn of the century clearly shows the Home Fleet at anchor north of Kirkwall.

This postcard was sent by Cecil Burton from Dover in 1912. He had just returned to Dover at 6 a.m. en route to Portsmouth after his ship HMS Jackal had attended the Royal Salute in Scapa Flow. He tells on this card how bad the weather was on the last leg of the journey south from Leith.

A sleepy Stromness located in north-western Scapa Flow, protected by a small ring of islands and the Island of Hoy in the distance. The fishing village, although used to the Royal Navy being in port, was unprepared for the arrival of the German High Seas battle Fleet in 1919.

from either aerial or naval attack, until the additional defence measures could be implemented. Lyness only became the centre of operations in 1919, after the war had ended.

Coastal defences were gradually increased to cover Hoxa, Switha and Hoy sounds and nineteen blockships were placed to cover the eastern approaches. These blockships were derelict or rusting, decommissioned hulks of merchantmen which were deliberately sunk to hamper access to Scapa Flow by enemy shipping. Submarine nets, steel pylons and minefields were also laid, as well as indicator loops which could detect submarine movements. Now that this increased system of defences was in place, the navy began to spend more time in Scapa Flow and the area became the principal training ground for ships and their crew before joining the Atlantic Fleet.

Action soon followed when early reconnaissance indicated that the German High Seas Fleet had put to sea on 30 May 1916. The Grand Fleet weighed anchor and left Scapa Flow, led by Admiral Jellico on his flagship the *Iron Duke*, with a fleet comprising of sixteen battleships. three battle cruisers, four armoured cruisers, five light cruisers and forty-four destroyers. He was joined by Admiral Sir David Beatty. Their combined forces greatly outnumbered the German Fleet by 144 ships to ninety-nine. The Battle of Jutland raged with twenty-five ships lost on both sides. Although the outcome was indecisive,

The inner harbour in Stromness, empty carts or horse-drawn carriages wait for either fish or munitions, as the harbour focus changed during the outbreak of war. The large building in the background is the Royal Hotel which was once the shore base offices for the Admiralty.

The St Ola, *seen here departing from Scapa Pier brought the mail to and from the islands as well as other vital stores and passengers. A new ferry terminal in Stromness now handles all of the island's traffic. It was from Scapa Pier that all of the fleet's business would be carried out.*

We rarely think of the lives at sea of the naval ratings and officers during those bleak war years and of the constant naval patrols undertaken to protect our shores and fleets. Christmas Greetings fly from the top mast of this British Navy Royal Sovereign class battleship.

with both sides claiming moral victories, the German fleet broke off the engagement and never again returned in force into the North Sea until their surrender in 1918.

Prior to this surrender, another German U-boat, the *UB-116*, penetrated the defences of Scapa Flow on 28 October 1918. She was detected by the indicator loops and allowed to proceed into the area of the controlled minefield, where she was blown up with the loss of thirty-seven men. It would be another twenty-one years before another U-boat was to enter Scapa Flow, this time successfully, resulting in the sinking of the *Royal Oak*.

2
The Loss of the *Hampshire*

The U-boat menace was still apparent in the North Sea and the eastern Atlantic, as many mines were laid to apprehend unwary shipping. The *Hampshire* left Scapa Flow on 5 June 1916, less than a week after the battle of Jutland, with Britain's Minister of War, Field Marshall Lord Kitchener and his staff. *En route* for Archangel in Russia to shore up Russia's defences against the increasing German threat, the 10,850-ton *Hampshire* headed into massive seas, against recommendations not to sail, until the bad weather had cleared. Shortly after

HMS Hampshire *left Scapa Flow on 5 June 1916 and blew up west of Marwick Point with a loss of 655 officers and men including, Britain's Minister of War, Field Marshall Lord Kitchener and his staff.*

Marwick Head, Birsay, Orkney.
Off this Headland H.M.S. Hampshire went down with Lord Kitchener and His Staff on Board.

Marwick Head is located on the west coast of Mainland between the small village of Marwick to the south and Birsay Bay to the north and can be reached on a spur road off the B9056. This peaceful scene belies the state of the weather when the Hampshire *set steam on that fateful day, as she headed into massive seas against recommendations not to sail until the bad weather had cleared.*

setting steam, the *Hampshire* blew up west of Marwick Point with the loss of 655 officers and men, only twelve seamen were to survive that day.

Great controversy ensued after the death of Lord Kitchener, as he had been openly criticized for his war tactics. The week prior to the *Hampshire* leaving Scapa Flow, the U-75 was known to have laid thirty-four mines in the vicinity. However, it is still unclear to this day whether the ship hit a mine or whether it was sabotaged by German, Irish or even British secret agents. This theory was further reinforced by the fact that the Stromness lifeboat was not allowed to attend the scene to look for survivors, locals attempting to help in a shore search were turned back at bayonet point and no potential witnesses were ever interviewed. Whatever the reasons for the tragic loss of this fine ship and all those men, the *Hampshire* now lies in 60m (200ft) of water off Marwick Head. A Memorial Tower to Lord Kitchener sits atop the cliffs near the scene of her loss.

Further rumours of sabotage proliferated when the *Vanguard* suddenly blew up on 9 July 1917 with a loss of over 700 lives. Lying north east of Flotta, witnesses tell of the massive explosion which occurred in the main magazine of the ship. Seemingly unstable ammunitions and cordite had ignited, setting off the main magazine. The remains of the *Vanguard* are now well broken up in 34m (114ft) of water. Recognizable sections are still apparent, but the ship is now classified as an official war grave, so no sport diving is allowed on her anymore.

The Earl Kitchener Memorial at Marwick Head.

LORD KITCHENER, K.G., K.P., G.C.B., etc.

Born June 24th 1850. Drowned by the sinking of H.M.S. Hampshire
off the Orkney Islands, June 5th, 1916.

Rest in Peace, Oh! warrior brave,
  Now your task is o'er;
All your best you gladly gave,
  To help us win the war.
But the "Last Post" now has sounded,
  You've laid aside your sword;
And God has called you from us,
  To your nobly won reward.
And this prayer we all are breathing,
  Though our hearts are wrung with pain:
Rest on in peace, brave soldier,
  Till the trumpet sounds again.

Opposite: Posted on 30 June 1916, just twenty-five days after Lord Kitchener was lost. He may have been a rather controversial figure, but his loss was felt dearly by the Nation. Another popular postcard at the time had a poem penned by Mr Lundy of Lundy and Doyle, the popular Irish comedians:

> Today the British Nation has with sorrow heard the news,
> Of one when duty called him did never once refuse;
> He was one of the greatest soldiers our country ever seen,
> He lost his life on duty for his country, king and queen.

A further verse stated:

> The Kaiser and his friends today are thinking all is well,
> But some day they will waken up to find themselves in hell

How prophetic that statement would be in 1919 when the first of the German Fleet arrived in Scapa Flow, which was regarded as a northern hell at the time.

HMS Vanguard, *seen here in Scapa Flow, was also at the centre of a mystery when her munitions suddenly exploded on 9 July 1917 with the loss of over 700 lives.*

While we were still at war, the propaganda machines were always hard at work. Here a German postcard is clearly showing that even although there is a mighty English blockade in the North Sea, German U-boats were striking at the heart of the enemy and succeeding in this rather stylized painting. The British Admiralty had another viewpoint on the matter. They were so sure of their overwhelming number of ships and of their success at the Battle of Jutland that the enemy were shown with the grass growing around their feet.

3

A Navy Surrenders

After the Battle of Jutland, the German Navy retired to its home ports of Wilhelmshaven and Kiel. Scheer was only to venture back to sea one more time before hearing once again that the British Navy was advancing on his fleet and he ordered his ships to disperse to their bases. In November of that same year, the fleet was ordered to break through the North Sea blockade and mutiny arose. Crews refused to set sail, or stokers to fuel the fires of the great ships. When Admiral von Hipper ordered the ships to disperse, mutiny spread from ship to ship and they came under the control of the Soviet of Workers, Soldiers and Sailors, a communist group who flew the red flag from each ship.

Finally, when the war was thought to be lost, those same communist sailors demanded peace, yet had to accept the orders from their previous officers (those who had not been killed by them during the mutiny) to sail the ships one last time. Under the terms of the armistice, in return for the lifting of the allied blockade of Germany, the Germans agreed to surrender the bulk of their navy. It was escorted to a position near the Firth of Forth where Admiral Sir David Beatty accepted the surrender from Rear-Admiral Meurer on board the ship *Königsberg*.

The German fleet surrendered officially on 21 November and sailed from Kiel and Wilhelmshaven where they were met by two columns of Allied ships, led by Vice-Admiral Madden on board the *Revenge* and Admiral Beatty on board the flagship *Queen Elizabeth*. First contact was made with the fleet, headed by the *Frederich der Grosse*, at 9.40 a.m. In all there were ten battleships, six battle cruisers, eight light cruisers, forty-nine destroyers and all their submarines. British officers and ratings at the time could not believe that the German fleet would come so quietly, yet here they were, supported by skeleton crews, without ammunition aboard, being led meekly towards the northern Orkney Islands and Scapa Flow.

The combined fleet reached Scapa Flow on 23 November and over the following week a total of seventy-four ships were interred, supported by a maintenance crew of 1,800 men. All other malcontents and mutineers (some 2,000 men) were shipped back to Germany on board the *Graf Waldersee* and *Sierra Ventana*. Admiral von Reuter was ultimately in charge of the interred German Fleet and he made the *Emden* his flagship.

Debilitated and demoralized, Von Reuter had a hard time keeping control of the German sailors, as technically the ships and men were only interred. They had not surrendered, as the terms of the peace treaty had still not been signed. In a letter sent from Admiral von Trotha, chief of the German Admiralty to Vice-Admiral von Reuter from Berlin in May 1919 it was stated:

> It appears that our opponents are considering the idea of depriving us of the interned ships on the conclusion of peace; they waver between the destruction or the distribution among themselves of these ships... I beg you, Sir, as far as possible to express to the officers and crews of the interned ships my satisfaction that, for their part, they are so eagerly awaiting our most natural hope, that the interned ships will be retained under the German Flag...it is to be hoped that they (German Delegates at the Peace Conference) will put an end to the internment which, through our enemies' breach of faith, has become so cruel, the sufferings and trials of which are deplored by our whole Navy, and which will be remembered to the credit of the interned crews.

The real fear was that the Allies would take control of the German High Seas Fleet and perhaps use the German Fleet against them should further conflict arise. Coupled with the mutinous control by the Communist Party of ships and ports, this was a dilemma which led Admiral Ludwig von Reuter to make one of the most important and most controversial decisions of his life. Britain was in favour of the ships' destruction, but France and the other allies were concerned about Britain's naval superiority and wanted the ships dispersed between themselves.

Published in Germany in 1915, this redrawn, rather stylized photograph shows the German High Seas Battle Fleet on manoeuvres in the North Sea, supported by aerial reconnaissance by dirigible. The two fleets would clash at the Battle of Jutland (known as the Battle of Skagerrak by the Germans) in May 1916. This photograph is of interest as it was taken from another accompanying hot air balloon and identifies a number of the ships which would later end up at the bottom of Scapa Flow.

Another interesting German aerial postcard of the Seydlitz *and* Hindenburg *engaged in a search pattern with a U-boat.*

After the German Navy surrendered and before their sailing to Scapa Flow was interred, the High Seas Battle Fleet were ordered to Kiel and Wilhelmshaven to off load their munitions and take on the necessary stores and skeleton crew to man the ships and prepare for a new life as caretakers, until the orders for the scuttling were issued.

This very rare postcard shows the names of the ships and their course northward. Never had there been seen so many naval warships together at any one time. It must have been quite a sight as all three fleets sailed north to Scapa Flow, both sides unsure of the other's intentions, unsure whether it may be a trap or a ploy to engage in further action. Their fears were finally settled when all of the ships reached their destination without further wartime incident.

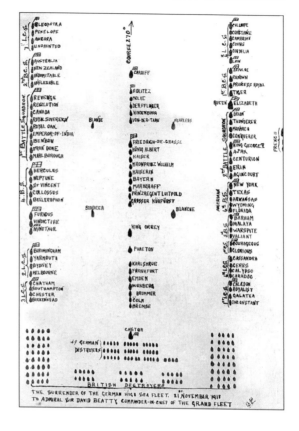

The German fleet surrendered officially on 21 November and sailed from Kiel and Wilhelmshaven, where they were met by the two columns of Allied ships led by Vice-Admiral Madden on board the Revenge and Admiral Beatty on the Queen Elizabeth.

SURRENDER OF GERMAN FLEET
KING'S VISIT TO THE QUEEN ELIZABETH PRIOR
TO THE SURRENDER OF THE GERMAN FLEET

The Queen Elizabeth *was the flagship of Admiral Beatty. Prior to the accepting the surrender of the German Fleet was visited by the King. As soon as preparations had been made and the British fleet were secure, they set sail to meet the German Fleet near the Firth of Forth, before continuing their way north to the Orkney Islands.*

The British Grand Fleet going out to meet The Vanquished German High Seas Fleet
At the Surrender *November 21st 1918.*
Copyright. 748. *Abrahams Devonport*

HMS Yarmouth *finally entered Scapa Flow on a cold and blustery day, leading the first of the German Light cruisers.*

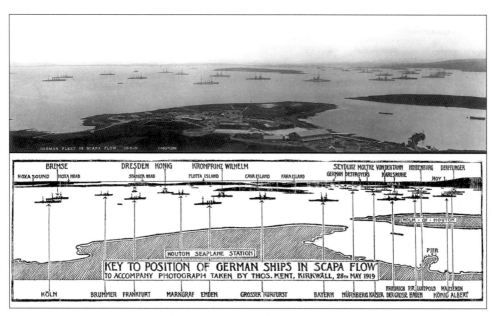

This panoramic view and accompanying artwork quite clearly show the exact position of the ships within Scapa Flow and their names. Photographed from the Naval Seaplane Station at Houghton, the view is south-east across Scapa Flow and was taken on 28 May 1919. Who would have realized that within three weeks, virtually the entire fleet would have been scuttled?

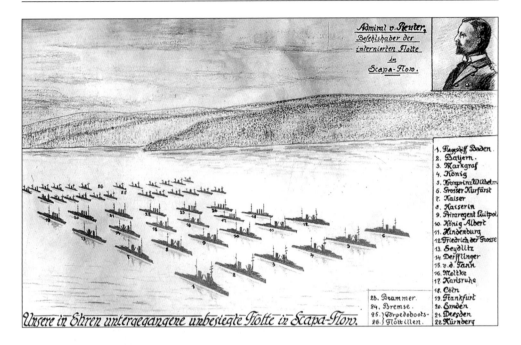

German postcards are indeed a rarity and it was quite a coup to discover two different aspects of the interred German Fleet settled in Scapa Bay. The inset shows a picture of Admiral von Reuter. There seems to be no other intention to the postcards other than creating a historical record of the internment, as no official German photographs were allowed to be taken, since technically both countries were still at war until the peace agreement had been signed.

Vice-Admiral Ludwig V. Reuter.

Admiral Von Trotha, Chief of the German Admiralty.

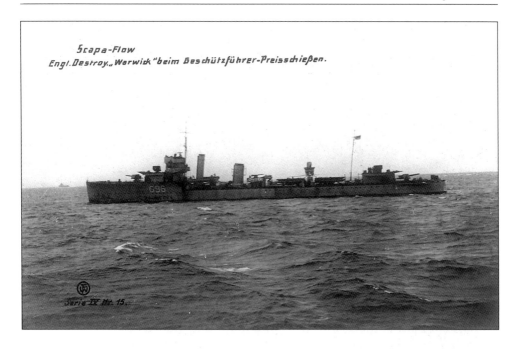

Scapa-Flow
Engl. Destroy. „Warwick" beim Geschützführer-Preisschießen.

I find it quite extraordinary that while British 'official' postcards were showing views of the German Fleet, German postcards at the time, published during the internment, only showed the British patrol vessels with incidental identification of the German Fleet in the background.

Scapa-Flow
Engl. Zerstörer Wallace

This and following page: *More of the German postcards from Scapa, focusing on the British rather than the German ships.*

Scapa-Flow
Engl. Zerstörer Wolstoen zwischen
Markgraf u. Bremse

Serie Ent. 12

Scapa-Flow
Engl. Post-Drifter „Lucy" klar zum Längseitgehen. Schiffe: Emden, Brummer, Bremse, Frankfurt, Cöln

Serie II Nr. 9

Two different views of the interred fleet. The German one simply says 'German Fleet in Scapa Flow'. However, the British card is more controversial, as it lists the German Fleet as 'spoils of war', which was very much untrue as nothing had been decided as to the fate of the ships, or indeed the outcome of any formal peace agreements.

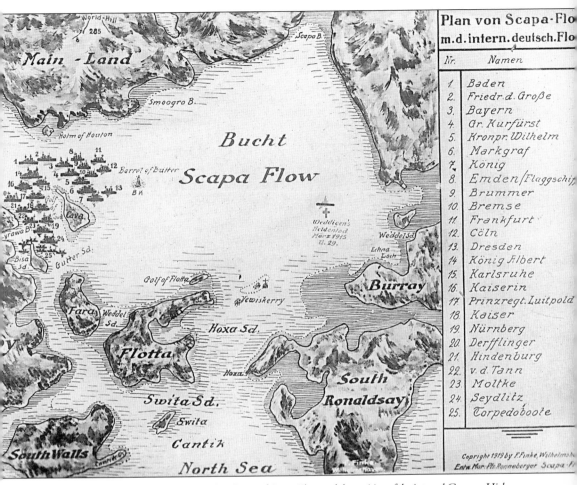

	Plan von Scapa-Flo m.d. intern. deutsch. Flo
Nr.	*Namen*
1.	Baden
2.	Friedr.d. Große
3.	Bayern
4.	Gr. Kurfürst
5.	Kronpr. Wilhelm
6.	Markgraf
7.	König
8.	Emden/Flaggschiff
9.	Brummer
10.	Bremse
11.	Frankfurt
12.	Cöln
13.	Dresden
14.	König Albert
15.	Karlsruhe
16.	Kaiserin
17.	Prinzregt. Luitpold
18.	Kaiser
19.	Nürnberg
20.	Derfflinger
21.	Hindenburg
22.	v.d. Tann
23.	Moltke
24.	Seydlitz
25.	Torpedoboote

Copyright 1919 by F.Finke, Wilhelmsh
Entw.Mar.-Pfr.Ronneberger Scapa-Fl

A very rare German Postcard showing a stylized map of Scapa Flow and the position of the interred German High Seas Fleet, published in 1919 in Wilhelmshaven.

The German battleship Kaiser *at anchor in Scapa Flow after its surrender.*

There are many similar and fine views of the German Fleet taken from the hills above Houghton, but this is of interest as they show that there was another side to the internment of the Fleet. Most people just think of the ships languishing in a somewhat relaxed manner within Scapa Bay, yet there were constant patrols and secure boom defences constantly manned by many naval patrol boats. It may have been hard on the Germans, but it was equally hard on the sailors and civilians engaged in the protection and supervision of the Fleet.

Hundreds of troops had to be relocated north to the Orkney Islands and needed ancillary services. New barracks had to be built at each of the bases, as well as a theatre, cinema, shops, laundry, canteens and transportation for both on the water and over land. It is fair to say that the Orkneys were inundated by military personnel whose lives would be changed irrevocably.

Photographed at Stromness Harbour this worthy squad of military shiprights and local carpenters and craftsmen were in constant work, erecting buildings, repairing machinery, handling cargoes and generally keeping the well-oiled wheels of post-war Britain running on time.

Bridge Street in Kirkwall is still a lively street, also paved in locally hewn slate. Here a naval rating in his uniform is quite clearly seen walking up the street. There are postcards for sale in the window of the shop to the left, they show views of the German Fleet at anchor, indicating that this photograph was posted in 1919.

Kirkwall also had squads of military personnel stationed in and around the town engaged in similar tasks. Here a cold, snowy day in the Orkneys, always necessitates layers of clothing and the military heavy serge uniforms at the time were perfect at keeping out the cold, but no good in the rain.

I love this old postcard. It takes a rather tongue-in-cheek view of the posting to the cold north. The Orkney posting was seen as possibly the worst going and there were some particularly scathing poems written about it at the time:

> This bloody town's a bloody cuss,
> No bloody trains, no bloody bus,
> And no one cares for bloody us,
> in bloody Orkney.
>
> All bloody clouds and bloody rain,
> No bloody kerbs, no bloody drains,
> The Council's got no bloody brains,
> In bloody Orkney.
>
> No bloody sport, no bloody games,
> No bloody fun, the bloody dames,
> Won't give their bloody names,
> In bloody Orkney.

4

Scuttled

Von Reuter had made plans as early as 1 June 1919 to scuttle the fleet, telling the officers on each of his ships to prepare all the seacocks and torpedo tubes and all other valves in readiness for his orders. The valves were to be prepared in such a way as to render them unable to be closed again. Signal flags were flown on 20 June to warn the crews to get ready and when the bulk of the Allied fleet left for exercise in the North Sea on the morning of 21 June, there remained only one British destroyer, the *Westcott*, left in Scapa Flow to guard the High Seas Fleet.

On the longest day of the year support craft, supply ships, soldiers, sailors and local Orcadians stood in shocked silence as the entire German High Seas Battle Fleet began to sink at the same time. Moored in parallel lines north of the Island of Cava and west of the Barrel of Butter buoy, the surprised crew of the supply ship *Trust On* were assailed by shouts of help and an appeal for the rescue of German sailors. In contravention of all orders all the German ships were flying their ensigns and battle flags, this was the last military action that these ships would ever see. Many of the smaller ships which were attached to each other were pulling each other down, the larger ships were either turning turtle or raising quickly by bow or stern. There was huge consternation in 'the Flow' to try and rescue all of the sailors before the fleet disappeared forever. Never before had such a sight been witnessed in all the years of naval combat.

Vice-Admiral Ludwig von Reuter said at the time:

> And what a scene it was! Before us, *Grosser Kürfurst* rose sharply into the air. With a racket both chains parted and the ship listed to port and capsized, the red paint of her bottom glaring across the blue sea… Of fifty ships, forty-six were sunk, a great performance! As I tried to reach them, English ships of the line rushed into the bay at top speed, ready for battle, their thirty-eight centimetre guns aimed at the remnant of my unit. It was time for me to visit the

The Emden, *awarded with the Iron Cross, was Von Reuter's flagship and it was from its foremast that his orders were given for the scuttling of the fleet. As a final retort, the red flag was raised on her stern, not now the communist flag of the insurrection, but the international code 'Z' which signalled 'Advance on the Enemy'.*

English admiral and effect the cessation of hostile action. The fire weakened and gradually stilled. In the background, the great cruisers were in their death-throes: *Seydlitz* capsized; the bulkheads and forecastles of *Derfflinger* and *Von Der Tann* were already flooded. They would soon be finished. Only *Hindenburg* lay flat upon the water, but she was settling.

In just over two hours, almost the entire German fleet had sunk. By the time the British Navy had returned to Scapa at 2.30 p.m. it was already too late. Violent scuffles arose when the last of the German ships were boarded in an attempt to halt their destruction. In the ensuing action two officers and six sailors were killed and a further five wounded.

The scuttling of the High Seas Fleet was in direct contravention of the terms of the Armistice. Subsequently von Reuter and his men were placed in custody as prisoners of war. The crews were sent to a military camp near Invergordon.

Salvage advisors arrived from the Navy on 24 June and after a thorough investigation it was decided that the ships could not be salvaged and that they were not a navigational hazard. Much of the wildlife above and below the waves and around the shoreline was killed due to the leaking oil when the ships sank.

The Aberdeen trawler *Ben Urie* ran aground on the hull of the *Moltke* in October 1920 and soon there were a number of letters of complaint about the rusting ships. Many trawlers ran aground, equipment got snagged on the wrecks and debris from the ships became a very real hazard, some of it floating over eighty miles away to the Banffshire coast. As peace reigned once more, the post-war industrial use for scrap metal rose and gradually greater interest was focused on the German Fleet in Scapa Flow.

Two very different views of the Bayern, *one taken shortly after her arrival at Scapa Flow and the other much more dramatic shot of her sinking on 21 June 1919.*

The German Battleship Markgraf *was one of the first battleships to turn turtle, the weight of her massive guns pulling the ship upside down as water filled her compartments.*

The König *and* Kronprinz Wilhelm *are in a similar condition. All are in very deep water and are regarded as the most serious dives in Scapa Flow, due to the extreme depth, limited time, reduced light and dangerous condition of the ships.*

A German battleship begins to succumb to the weight of water it is taking on (above). Below, a destroyer is even closer to a watery grave.

When the Moltke *rolled over, she presented an immediate navigation hazard and it was not long before she was hit by another ship. Here the whaler* Ramna *was stranded high and dry when the tide went out. A number of the smaller cruisers were run aground before they could sink. This is a wonderful view of two German cruisers high and dry on the shores of Scapa Flow.*

Madness reigned for those brief minutes when the crew from capsizing ships took to their life rafts. The British Admiralty were completely taken by surprise and some were even unaware that the ships were sinking, ordering the German sailors to return to their ships at gun point. However, it soon became clear that there was no return for the men, or their ships.

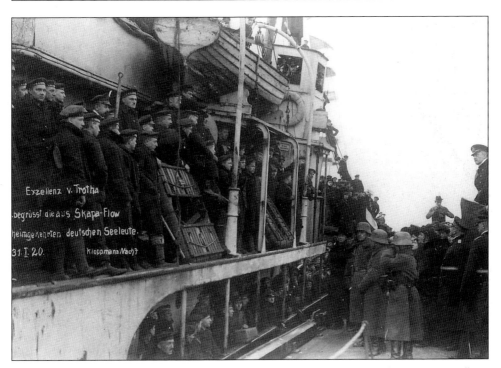

Exzellenz v. Trotha
.begrüsst die aus Skapa-Flow
heimgekehrten deutschen Seeleute.
31.I.20.   Kloppmann/Nacht

After several months in POW camps the German sailors were eventually repatriated. Here His Excellency Admiral von Trotha, commanding officer in charge of the Internment Fleet, is welcoming the German sailors returning from Scapa Flow on 31 January 1920.

5

Salvaging A Navy

Illegal salvage and wrecking operations were soon to start around Scapa Flow. With such an abundance of booty lying at their doorsteps, local Orcadians could not pass up the chance for looting and stripping down everything which lay above water level. Finally, the first salvage company, Stromness Salvage Syndicate, was formed in 1922 and purchased the destroyer *G89* which had been beached on Cava. The vessel was refloated, taken to Stromness and dismantled. The rusting hull was eventually sold for £50 to Cox & Danks in 1928 as a counter-weight to be used in the salvage of the *Seydlitz*. In close connection with the United Kingdom Salvage Company of Glasgow, Mr J.W. Robertson formed the Scapa Flow Salvage and Shipbreaking Company in 1923 and initially bought four destroyers, all in shallow water, from the navy. These ships were part of the compliment sunk near the naval base at Lyness. Using a combination of two concrete barges, spanned by heavy steel girders, a series of slings were constructed and placed under the German destroyers, forming a lifting cradle. As the tide dropped, the hawsers were pulled tight by a series of pulleys and little by little the ships were raised, taking them to shallow water where they could again be beached and scrapped.

However, before his first destroyer could be lifted, a rival operation had moved into Scapa Flow. Cox & Danks Ltd purchased twenty-six destroyers and two battleships from the Admiralty in 1924. Moving their base of operation to Lyness in Scapa Flow from the Thames was no mean feat, as they had to transport all their equipment and men, two ex-Admiralty towing tugs, the *Ferrodanks* and the *Sinodian* and a German floating dock, which had ironically been given to Britain as part of the payment for the illegal sinking of the High Seas Fleet. The Cox & Danks dock was capable of lifting a dead weight of 3,000 tons, but before the 700 mile journey north to the Orkney Islands could be undertaken, it was fitted out with £40,000 of equipment, including air compressors, generators, railway tracks, crane jibs, workshops, lifting wires, steel beams, hawsers, winches and all other possible materials and men which

The German battleship Baden *is raised by the floating dock of Cox & Danks Ltd.*

could be employed in this massive venture. They took a gamble visiting Scapa Flow. The Admiralty had issued a statement that the deeper battleships could not be salvaged economically. However, they decided to press ahead with the venture. On a further inspection of Scapa Flow, they were so convinced of the enterprise that they also purchased the battleships *Moltke* and *Von Der Tann*, the battlecruisers *Kaiser* and *Prinzregent Luitpold* and the light cruiser *Bremse*.

Employing the same method laid out by Mr Robertson, they cut the floating dock in two, effectively making two barges. Cables were slung under the ships to be salved and the winches were wound in by hand, gradually lifting the ships to be towed into shallow water and dismantled. They successfully raised twenty-five ships by this method. Once started of course, they learned a great deal about the construction of naval ships, especially the larger battleships and battlecruisers. On further consultation with Admiralty architects Cox & Danks decided on a revolutionary form of salvage by pumping compressed air into the ships' hulls. To enable this technique to work effectively, huge towers were constructed on the sunken ship's hull containing pressure locks. Once sealed onto the deck, compressed air was pumped into the towers expelling the sea water and making it possible for divers to climb down inside the towers and enter the ship through the air locks. Utilizing existing air-tight pockets, the divers further sealed off all other hatchways, companionways, decks and windows to make the ship watertight and airtight once more and compressed air was pumped in.

Diving equipment was bought from Siebe-Gorman & Co. Ltd, the world leaders at the time. Their 'open' diving suit, first pioneered in 1819 and based on the principal of the diving bell was thought to be too difficult for the job on the shipwrecks, so their 'closed' diving apparatus was used. This was a heavy brass helmet which screwed onto a neck ring and breast plate which fitted over a sealed suit, further weighted down by massive lead-filled boots. Air was pumped into the helmet by an umbilical hose with line attached. A second valve on the helmet was for expired air which was controlled manually by the diver. This allowed the diver to control the amount of air in the suit, and giving it a certain level of buoyancy. A series of pressure gauges told the operators of the air pump how deep the diver was, what pressure he was working at and what pressure of air was required to keep him alive. The helmet was fitted with a glass viewing port which quite often steamed up and had to be cleaned by way of the 'spit valve'. This was a small valve which allowed sea water to come into the helmet, then the diver took a mouth full of water to spit onto the face plate to keep it clear.

The first ship to be raised by this method was the *Moltke*, which lay in 21m (70ft) of water. The 22,640-ton battleship was raised on 10 June 1927, beached on Cava and then towed to Lyness where all of her heavy machinery was removed through her hull in readiness for the long journey south to the dock yards at Rosyth in the Firth of Forth, north of Edinburgh. The *Seydlitz*, at 25,000 tons, was the next to be raised on 3 November 1927, followed by the 24,500 ton *Kaiser* on 20 March 1929 and the *Bremse* weighing only 4,000 tons on 27 November that same year.

The Seydlitz, seen here before the German surrender (probably after the Battle of Jutland), was purchased by Cox & Danks and raised in November 1927.

Once sufficient air pressure had built up in the hull of the sunken vessel, the ship floated back up to the surface, rising faster as the air expanded under the decreasing ambient pressure causing the ships to literally launch themselves through the surface of the water like a great breaching whale. Here the Derfflinger was the last ship to be raised. At a weight of 28,000 tons and from a depth of 45m it was an incredible feat of engineering salvage at work.

A German battleship floating bottom-up after being pumped full of air.

After a failed bid to raise the *Hindenburg* in 1927, it was finally pumped full of air and raised on an even keel on 22 July 1930. Unlike the other battleships and battle cruisers which were towed to the Forth upside down, the *Hindenburg* was the first ship to be towed upright. Cox & Danks used their own three salvage ships for the arduous task. That same year on 7 December, the *Von der Tann* was raised. The last ship to be raised by the partnership of Cox & Danks was the *Prinzregent Luitpold* on 9 July 1931. The price of scrap had fallen to an all time low and Cox & Danks sold their share to the Alloa Company, which had been responsible for shifting the scrap. The company was later renamed Metal Industries.

After being in business just nine months, Metal Industries raised their first ship by the compressed air method on 5 September 1934. The 28,000-ton battleship *Bayern* was raised from 36m (120ft) with air locks over 27m (90ft) long. While the work of stripping the ship down at Lyness continued, work also began on the *König Albert* which rested in 41m (138ft). The airlocks were removed from the *Bayern*, extended another 3m (10ft) and fitted onto the upturned hull of the *König Albert*. It took another eight months work before the ship floated free and hit the surface on 31 August 1935.

Over the next three years, Metal Industries successfully raised the 25,000-ton battleship *Kaiserin*, the 25,000-ton battleship *Frederich der Grosse* (reaching an all-time scrap record of £150,000), the 25,000 ton battleship *Grosser Kürfurst* and finally the *Derfflinger* at 28,000 tons, one of the largest ships ever raised and certainly from the deepest water at 45m (150ft).

Metal Industries continued their presence in Scapa Flow at their base at Lyness until March 1947 when they finally withdrew to their depot at Faslane on the Clyde estuary. They sold their salvage rights to the German Fleet in 1956 to Nundy Marine Metals, owned by Arthur Nundy who had been one of the chief salvage divers working for Metal Industries. Mr Nundy sold his salvage rights to Scapa Flow Salvage in 1972. Only seven (fairly intact) of the scuttled German Fleet remain and it is those ships which still attract so much interest. There are three 26,000-ton battleships, the *König*, *Markgraf* and the *Kronprinz Wilhem*, there are also four light cruisers weighing between 4,000 and 6,000 tons each, the *Karlsrühe*, *Brummer*, *Dresden* and the *Köln*.

No. 1   GERMAN BATTLE CRUISER "HINDENBURG" AS SHE NOW RESTS   COPYRIGHT. C. W. BURROWS
AT SCAPA, 21-6-1919

The Hindenburg *and* Von Der Tann *were both successfully raised from the seabed by Cox & Danks. It would be a further fourteen months before the* Bayern *would be raised by Metal Industries.*

BAYERN.

1. *Part of the original oakleaf and crown from the* Royal Oak *nameplate, salvaged by Orcadian divers.*

2. *Gravestones from the* Royal Oak *in the naval cemetery at Lyness on the Island of Hoy.*

3. The Battle Ensign, newly attached by the Elite Royal Navy Northern Diving Group, is flown from the propeller shaft of the stricken Royal Oak *before being made secure for its year-long vigil on the wreck.*

4. One of the many wreaths laid at sea each year in the waters of Scapa Flow. This message by Don Harris, one of the original survivors, reads 'They Gave Their Todays, So That We Could Have Our Tomorrows'.

5. *A Royal Navy diver does the final preparation of his oxygen rebreather set before venturing into the cold waters for the annual inspection of HMS* Royal Oak. *The initials SNICDU stand for the Scotland and Northern Ireland Clearance Diving Unit, which has now been renamed the Northern Diving Unit.*

6. *This air-diving Royal Navy team member is being helped on with his equipment. Note the inverted air tanks on his back and the buoyancy air bottle attached to his rubberized dry suit. Nose clips, full face mask, weightbelt, fins, knife, torch and buoy line make up the rest of the equipment.*

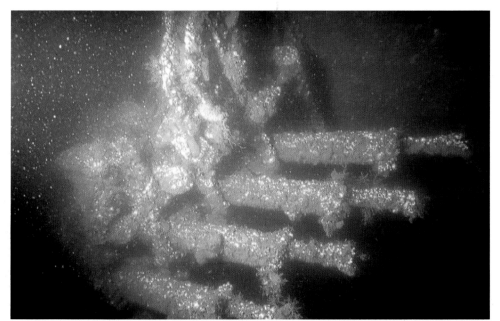

7. *The anti-aircraft guns are still in place with full magazines of shells attached. They never had a chance to fire in retaliation against the sudden and catastrophic attack on the* Royal Oak.

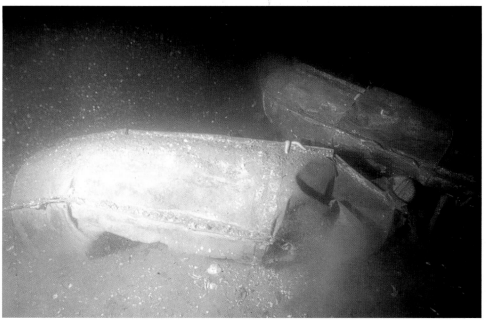

8. *Carley life rafts litter the seabed under the upturned hull of the Royal Oak. Many of them had been damaged during their last manoeuvres in the North Sea and could not be used to rescue the men from the rapidly sinking ship.*

9. *A diver hangs suspended in the water over the remaining gun turret on the* Köln. *The* Köln *is one of the most popular wrecks of the German High Seas Fleet.*

10. The bridge railings from the Dresden are now covered in all manner of marine life such as feather starfish, sea squirts and soft corals.

11. Here a diver equipped with a very necessary light explores the port side of one of the sunken German cruises.

12. The once cavernous interior of the Inverlane *in the Burra Sound is no longer safe for divers as the ship has collapsed.*

13. Remains of the blockship Doyle *in Burra Sound, now festooned with kelp. You can only dive the blockships at slack water each day due to the strength of the tidal stream.*

14. *A diver approaches the bows of one of the blockships in Scapa Flow, listing heavily to port. The hull is covered in plumose anemones and topped with kelp. The diver only has a short time before the relentless movement of the tide forces him to abandon his exploration of the wreck.*

15. One of the Scapa Flow dive boats sits in the early morning foggy calm over one of the sunken German Fleet as the on board divers ready themselves for their exploration.

16. *Inside the hull of the* Gobernador Bories, *this diver pauses for my photograph before continuing his exploration out of the strong current which constantly lashes these blockships.*

17. Part of the superstructure of the Köln lies collapsed in on itself on the seabed.

18. The Admiral's steam pinnace was attached to the Royal Oak when she was sunk and was dragged under the waves, unable to assist in the rescue of the men that fateful night.

19. The gravestone of one of the few German sailors who were killed during the intentional sinking of the High Seas Fleet by Ludwig von Reuter.

20. Now high and dry beside the Churchill Barrier Number 4 at Water Sound, this blockship was part of the first attempts to block enemy shipping from passing into Scapa Flow.

21. *St George and the Dragon, constructed from concrete by the Italian prisoners of war, now rests in front of the Italian Chapel on Lamb Holm.*

22. *The interior of the Italian Chapel today, beautifully restored by the original artist Domenico Chiocchetti. It is a special place of pilgrimage for everyone visiting the Orkney Islands.*

23. *With the tidal stream racing in the background, this diver emerges from the water onto the support of the dive boat, having successfully completed a dive on the blockships in Burra Sound.*

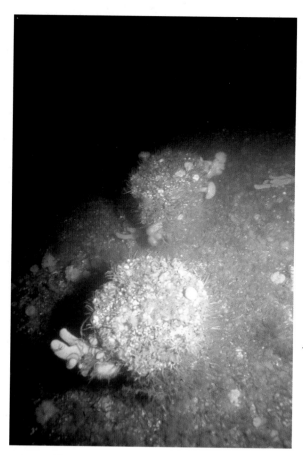

24. These bollards from the Köln ? are now covered in starfish, anemones and soft corals – called 'Dead Man's fingers'.

25. A modern aerial view of the Churchill Barriers, looking over the route which Günther Prien used to gain entry into Scapa Flow on 13 October 1939.

VON DER TANN.

The Hindenburg *was so large and moored in such shallow water that when she sank all of her top superstructure remained above the water level, leaving her open to local souvenir hunters.*

HINDENBURG.

Similar scenes were being enacted all over Scapa Flow. Here the Seydlitz, at 25,000 tons, was the second ship to be raised by Cox & Danks on 3 November 1927. Holes were cut into her hull and she was floated upside down and towed to Rosyth dry dock where she was scrapped. The Derfflinger sank within minutes of the Seydlitz, but she turned out to be one of the most difficult to be raised due to the extreme depth and size of the ship.

PUBLISHED BY
AERIAL PHOTO CO.,
PETERBOROUGH.

Nº228.   GERMAN BATTLE CRUISER "SEYDLITZ"
SUNK AT SCAPA FLOW, JUNE 1919.

COPYRIGHT.
SADLER & RENOUF.

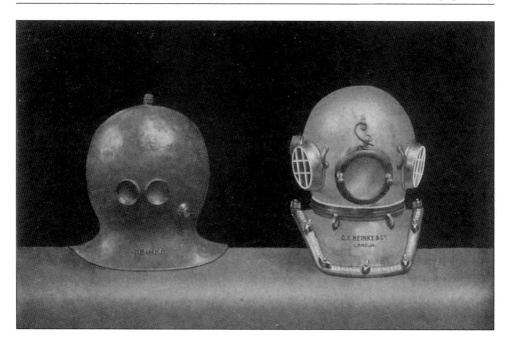

The salvage operations in Scapa Flow were also seen as a huge commercial opportunity for all types of supply companies and in particular those companies involved in the manufacture of diving equipment, as it would be the hard hat divers who would lead the way to the successful salvage of the ships.

These divers were incredibly brave, weighted down and fed air by means of a pump from a support vessel overhead. It was the divers' duty to seal all the holes in the ships, close compartments and fit the huge air 'funnels' to the hulls of the scuttled fleet, so that entry could be made and air pumped into the ships to raise them off the seabed.

A commercial diver drops down into the water over the unturned hull of one of the sunken ships. His umbilical air pipe and attachment ropes are trailing behind him.

The small diving support boat is dwarfed by the exposed superstructure of a German battleship.

No. 10   SALVAGE PARTY WORKING ON A GERMAN DESTROYER   COPYRIGHT. C. W. BURROW

A salvage party is hardly what I would call these sailors. The ship was the Hindenburg *and for many years she lay with her upper portion clear of the water line. These sailors are relieving her of any movable objects which could later be bartered in town. The* Hindenburg *was the only battleship to be refloated in her normal position on 22 July 1930.*

SALVING GERMAN BATTLESHIP

Members of the Cox & Danks' salvage team on board one of the raised destroyers, seaweed and other marine life still clinging to the now dry decks. The lowest paid workers or manual labourers would be denoted by their cloth flat caps, foremen would have a type of bowler hat or wide-brimmed hat so that they could be recognized, even at great distance.

Victoria Street in Stromness with its street decked in huge paving slabs cut from locally-quarried slate. The Stromness Museum at the end of this street houses an excellent display of memorabilia from the sinking of the German Fleet with many artefacts recovered from the wrecks by visiting divers.

SUNKEN GERMAN FLEET "SCAPA FLOW" 1926.

The Moltke was the obvious first choice for the salvors, as her hull was well above the water line. Cox & Danks cut away the armoured steel plating, filled her with air, built support sheds on top fitted with air compressors and had her towed to the dry docks at Rosyth.

CUTTING INTO BATTLESHIP MOLTKE.

Four different, yet dramatic postcard views of the salvage operations in Scapa Flow in the late 1920s. The determination of these companies and the salvaging of the warships was nothing less than spectacular. Huge sums of money were paid for the scrap metal, especially by a country that was about to enter another war and needed the

GUNS OF SALVED GERMAN BATTLESHIP SCAPA, FLOW.

raw material to construct ships and tanks. It is somewhat ironic that the largest salvage platform was also German and helped to scrap German ships, the metal from which would be later used against that same country. Just what deals were being made then?

SALVING GERMAN BATTLESHIP SCAPA FLOW.

A German battleship sits in a Rosyth dock after being towed from Scapa Flow.

A contemporary advert by Briggs & Sons Co. proving that their paint had been exported to Germany and used on the hulls of the striken vessels to great effect. What an advert!

6

Diving the German
High Seas Fleet

The invention of the aqualung, or demand valve, by Jacque Yves Cousteau and Pierre Gagnan, and the huge advances in modern diving technology have enabled sports divers or scuba divers to explore the remaining sunken ships with relative ease (SCUBA stands for Self Contained Underwater Breathing Apparatus). Safe diving practice and proper deep-dive training ensure that visiting divers to the Orkney Islands are able to enjoy these wonderful ships within safe diving limits of depth and time and thus avoid the crippling bends.

The diving to be undertaken in Scapa Flow is indeed serious and can be best categorized from two different aspects. Virtually all of the German fleet are in waters of 30m (100ft) or more which means that time is limited to dive the ship safely within decompression limits. Due to the depth, there is less light penetration, as there is little current resulting in more suspended particulate in the water. This generally means that it is never very clear on the wrecks and it will take several dives on each ship to get your bearings. The blockships are another matter, they are all sunk in fairly shallow water of 15m (50ft) or less, giving you ample bottom time to explore the ships fully. Due to the current, particularly on an incoming tide, the water is also remarkably clear. However, there is a down side to this, as the best blockships to dive are positioned in an area of extreme current, presenting the visiting diver with only limited time to dive the ships safely in slack water.

Thankfully, the owners and skippers of the dive boats which operate in Scapa Flow are all very knowledgeable of the tides and the positions of the ships. When starting your dive trip, it is best to start on one of the shallower German wrecks such as the *Karlsrühe*. As the water is generally considered too deep to undertake two dives on the German fleet in the same day, the usual dive plan is to dive a deep wreck first and then a second much shallower dive on one of the blockships or shallower wrecks near Lyness or Cava, such as the *F2* and its attendant barge or the *Roedean*. The *Roedean*, formerly known as the *Roebuck*, sank as a result of dragging her anchor in 1915 and struck the *Imperieuse*. However, the official line is that she struck a mine and sank. She was blasted apart twice in the 1950s to give suitable clearance over her decks.

That is also not to say that wreck diving is the only worthwhile diving to do in the Orkney Islands. There are superb scenic dives on underwater reefs and subterranean cliffs that are covered in a profusion of marine life. Diving outside Scapa Flow is always in crystal-clear water and is so underrated. It is difficult to understand the attraction of a lot of old rusting hulks on the seabed.

The F2 was a German escort boat similar to a light cruiser and was built at the Germaniawerft shipyard in Kiel and was completed in 1936. Converted to a torpedo recovery vessel, she displaced 756 tons and was 75m long (263ft). Captured during the Second World War, she sank at her mooring in Gutter Sound in 1946. A subsequent salvage operation to raise her 20mm guns failed when the barge used also sank alongside the ship. Both ships make an excellent dive in 18m of water (60ft).

Much of the metal plating has now fallen off and corroded away from the former bridge of the F2, leaving only the 'skeleton' rib.

The forward gun of the F2 is still intact and gives visiting divers an impression of her firing power.

Now trailing marine growth, this other view of the bridge of the F2 can be easily explored. However, divers should beware of the possibility of becoming entangled.

The crumpled stern with the propeller already removed by salvors now lies in 20 metres of water near the former Naval Base at Lyness.

Karlsrühe

Launched in 1916, the *Karlsrühe* was a second-class cruiser of the Königsberg II-class and four sister ships. Powered by 45,000 horsepower, geared turbines, the warship was capable of speeds over twenty-eight knots, making her a very effective ship in battle conditions. The *Karlsrühe* was 149m long and weighed 5,354 tons. At full battle stations, she had a ship's compliment of 500 men and carried eight 5.9in guns.

Due to her geographic position within Scapa Flow, the wreck is swept by a light current of around a half knot, keeping the waters in this area clearer than any of the other German wrecks. Now lying in a north-westerly direction on her starboard side the entire midships are pretty well broken up, but with a maximum depth of 24-27m to the seabed and only 12-14m to the uppermost deck; the wreck is popular with divers. The midship section was destroyed by salvage divers intent on getting into the ship by the easiest way possible, but the bows and stern are still intact. The stern is the most interesting with the wooden deck now at ninety degrees to the seabed. A steam capstan, mooring bollards and one of the guns are still attached. As you swim along the seabed towards the bows, you can see much debris from the blasting including the masts, bits of the three funnels, twisted steel plates and a mass of tangled spars and other unrecognizable metal bits. The bows are intact and the starboard anchor chain is visible.

SMS Karlsrühe.

Brummer

Originally designed in 1913, the *Brummer* finally joined the German fleet in the autumn of 1916. She was capable of carrying 360 mines and had only four 5.9in guns all mounted on the ship's centreline and a further two 3.4in anti-aircraft guns mounted behind the last funnel. She displaced 4,308 tons and was 139m long. The *Brummer* was powered by two turbine engines, each controlling its own propeller, working in tandem they were capable of powering the ship to an incredibly fast thirty-four knots.

Now lying on her starboard side in a maximum depth of 36m in a north-westerly direction, the ship is still in very good condition and extremely popular with divers. It is mostly intact, save for a wrecked section near the stern and another smaller wrecked area caused by salvors near the bow, the shallowest part of the upturned port deck is in 20m. The underside of the bow is totally smothered in plumose anemones, the top of the port side of the ship is covered in small, brittle starfish, sea urchins, small sponges, spider crabs and even pipe fish. Where there were once portholes, the holes are now ringed in soft corals called dead man's fingers.

The mid section of the superstructure is now collapsed in on itself, making it more hazardous to swim through, but inspection of all the holes and companionways is always rewarding, yet sometimes disconcerting with the ship lying on its side. The interior of the ship is virtually pitch black and dive lights are recommended at all times. Further penetration of the ships is not recommended as a number of divers have met untimely deaths lost in the maze of passageways. Swimming along the mast, the now vertical deck there is a single 150mm (5.9in) gun forward and aft. Sadly, much of the mid section is totally destroyed, blasted apart by the indiscriminate use of explosives by salvors.

Dresden

The *Dresden* was built at the Howaldtswerke Dockyard in Kiel and launched on 25 April 1917. Identical to the *Köln*, her name *Dresden* was the signature make for the Dresden II class of light cruiser. She was 153m long (510ft) and displaced 5,531 tons. Coal and oil fired she was capable of over twenty-seven knots. Although she was identical in construction to the *Köln*, her gun positions either side of the bridge were changed to the lower deck. The ship was also capable of carrying 200 mines which could be launched off the stern.

Due to a previous action with a British submarine, the *Dresden* had been holed and was still undergoing repairs at Stettin on the Baltic when the navy surrendered. She finally limped to Scapa Flow on 6 December, almost three weeks after the rest of the fleet had taken up anchor in the Orkneys.

The light cruiser Brummer.

The light cruiser Dresden, *identical in build to the* Köln *but with relocated gun positions.*

She quickly sank on 21 June, joining her sister ship *Köln* and now lies on her port side facing west of north, with her bows in approximately 30m and her stern sloping down to 38m. Almost intact, the *Dresden* is a very popular dive with divers, particularly the stern section which still has her two 150mm guns. The shallowest part of the wreck is in 16-18m where divers can orient themselves by connecting the shot line to the marker buoy on the surface. The entire outer superstructure of the hull is a mass of anemones, sponges and soft corals. Up forward, the guns have been salvaged, but the bridge is still fairly intact with the foremast now lying on the seabed. The mid-section has again been completely destroyed by the salvors. The stern is perhaps the most interesting from a photographic viewpoint, but the sharp bow rising up above the seabed at 34m still takes a bit of beating as one of the best views of the sunken fleet.

The German light cruiser on her port side is now disintegrating at an alarming rate after more than eighty years on the seabed.

A diver passes over the port rail of the Dresden.

The port railings and smaller guns of the Dresden *are particularly distinctive for visiting divers.*

Köln

The *Köln* was built in Hamburg by Blohm und Voss and entered into service in 1918. She was a Dresden II class light cruiser and was built along near identical lines to her sister ship the *Dresden*. With two sets of turbines driving two propellers, this class of warship was a formidable adversary and the British Admiralty were delighted when they were handed over as part of the internment fleet. At battle stations, the ship required 559 officers and men, but when she sailed to Scapa Flow, there was just a skeleton crew to look after the ill-fated ship. Commanded by Captain Heinemann, when the orders came to scuttle the ship, he quickly took action by destroying all of the sea cocks. The ship heeled over and sank at 1.50 p.m. on that same Saturday. Heinemann and his crew took off their caps which displayed the ship's name and joining other evacuees from the *Brummer* which went down in a similar fashion, surrendered to the British Navy.

The *Köln* now lies in 34m of water, her bows pointing in a north-westerly direction. The shallowest part of the port side deck is in 21m, as the ship now rests on her starboard side. Her stern gun is still in place and apart from a huge, gaping hole near the stern, the ship is in excellent shape and is regarded as one of the most popular by visiting divers. One of the classic views of the *Köln* is looking upwards towards the empty lifeboat davits and the 150mm guns which have lost their outer cylindrical housing. There are rows of portholes all along the upturned hull, each one offering a glimpse of the dark interior.

The Köln, *a Dresden II class light cruiser.*

This anchor is still in place on the upturned hull and is covered in soft corals called Dead Man's Fingers.

The smaller gun batteries are still in place on most of the scuttled German light cruisers and are a delight for divers to see.

A classic view upwards on the Köln of the former 150mm gun which has now lost its cylindrical casing.

Encrusted in marine growth, this bollard is 'settling' into the rotting wooden decks of this stricken ship.

König

The *König* is one of three remaining battleships of the original eleven which were left to rot on the seabed of Scapa Flow. Built by Kaiserliches Werft at Wilhelmshaven she joined the German High Seas Fleet in August 1914. Displacing 25,388 tons, the ship was over 172m long (575ft) and was powered with three coal/oil-fired turbines, each one driving a single propeller to a maximum speed of 23 knots. Once the flagship of the Battle Fleet during the Battle of Jutland, the ship is perhaps one of the more disappointing dives.

When sea water rushes into a ship, it alters the buoyancy and thus affects how the ship may settle on the seabed. The *König* was so top heavy, it had five twin turrets, each holding two 300mm guns (8in) weighing around 600 tons each, that the shift in her stability was such that the she turned turtle, her guns swung free and hit the soft clay substrate at 40m, driving her guns and superstructure into the mud.

The shallowest part of the upturned hull is in 20m and when you descend to the intact part of the hull, it is just like approaching the seabed, as there is much

'A German Greeting.' This postcard shows the *König* in its proud years as the flagship of the German Battle Fleet.

89

low encrusting marine life and that ever pervading cloud of silt which follows the unwary diver whose fin kicks come too close to the ship. However, here the similarity ends, as much of the hull has been blasted open by various salvors over the years to gain access to the non-ferrous metals in the engine rooms. Many divers still penetrate the inner areas of the ship from these sections, but it is considered highly dangerous and unsafe. The risk of snagging your equipment is high, as there are so many jagged, indistinguishable bits of wreckage everywhere.

With her bows facing approximately south-east there is now only a small area of the ship clear on her starboard side where part of her secondary casement armaments can be seen. Cold and dark at 40m, the visiting diver has little time to come to terms with this once massive battleship and all too soon you have to make the journey back up to the surface.

Kronprinz Wilhelm

The *Kronprinz Wilhelm* was built by Krupps shipyard in Kiel and joined the Third Battle Squadron of the High Seas Fleet in January 1915. Originally named the *Kronprinz*, she was the last of the König Class dreadnoughts to be completed and required over 1,100 men to keep her at battle stations. With a top speed of over twenty-one knots, the *Kronprinz Wilhelm* saw action several times and for the most part remained unscathed until she received a torpedo hit from the British submarine *J1*. Suitably repaired, her next action involved a collision with the *Grosser Kürfurst* and was again out of commission.

She was renamed *Kronprinz Wilhelm* on the fifty-nineth birthday of Kaiser Wilhelm on 27 January 1918. At the end of the war, when the terms for internment were being completed, the ship languished for over seven months before setting off for Scapa Flow.

The *Kronprinz Wilhelm* is perhaps the most accessible of the three battle ships, with the shallowest part of the upturned hull in only 14m of water, allowing divers a little more time to decompress on the ship before returning to light and warmth above. Now settled at an angle on her starboard side, her superstructure and main guns are also embedded in the seabed 34m below, but here the ship hit hard shale under the soft mud and much of the upturned port side of the ship is accessible to divers.

There are three main holes in her hull where the salvors blasted their way into the stern, the engine rooms and the bows. Again, the intact hull resembles the seabed, but everyone drops down the port side of the ship into the increasing gloom to try and discern recognizable aspects of the battleship. Gun turrets are always an obvious target. The huge mainmast that snapped off at the base, lies out at ninety degrees to the ship is still fairly intact with its now crushed spotting top. The scale of the ship is simply mind boggling and divers return time after time to continue exploring this wonderful old battleship.

Markgraf

Built by A.G. Weser at Bremen, the *Markgraf* was built to the same specifications as the *König* and *Kronprinz Wilhelm*. She joined the High Seas Fleet in 1914 and her first action was during the battle for the Baltic Islands in 1917. Also weighing 25,388 tons, the ship was over 172m long (575ft) and was powered by three triple-stage Parsons turbines, each one driving a single propeller to a maximum speed of twenty-one knots. Over 1,100 officers and ratings were needed to keep this battleship at action stations, as her armaments included a massive array of firepower including, five underwater torpedo tubes, capable of launching 50cm torpedoes packed with 250kg of explosive.

Sadly, the *Markgraf's* commanding officer Korvettenkapitan Walther Schumann was shot dead by a Royal Marine when the ship was boarded in an effort to stop the battleship sinking. His grave is in the Naval Cemetery at Lyness on the Island of Hoy. Interestingly, it was the imprisoned crew of the *Markgraf* which incited the first riots in Kiel by the mutineers which brought about the end of Imperial Germany. The *Markgraf* is perhaps considered to be the most serious of all the sunken ships, as the seabed depth is 46m (153ft). Lying west-north-west, the ship is also upside down with the shallowest part of the starboard hull at 22m.

The ship has bedded in on her port side and apart from the massive hole forward and at either side where her former torpedo tubes were once located near the stern, the hull is remarkably intact. It is under her starboard side that the old teak deck shines in your torch light and the now silent guns are covered in all manner of marine life. This is a memorable dive and not to be missed on any trip.

7

The Bull

On 12 October 1939, a month after war had been declared, the Prime Minister, Mr Neville Chamberlain, rejected Adolf Hitler's peace proposals in terms which made it clear that Britain would fight to the end.

Even while Hitler was brokering a peace, German naval expansion was accelerated immediately. The invasion of Norway was investigated and plans were already being drawn up for the invasion of Holland and Belgium – *Fall Gelb* (Case Yellow). It had always been in Commodore Dönitz's mind to avenge what had happened in the First World War at Scapa Flow. It was discussed many times within Fleet Headquarters. The final convincing came from Dönitz's staff operations officer Lt Cdr Öhrn who, after studying the charts once more said with firmness of character: 'I think it will be possible to find a way of penetration'.

The latest Luftflotte 2 (2nd Air Fleet) flight reconnaissance ordered by Commodore Dönitz on 11 September and then again on 26 September 1939 had shown that almost the entire British Fleet lay at anchor in Scapa Flow. Right from the beginning of the war Dönitz had demanded a survey of Scapa Flow by the *Seekriegsleitung*, the staff responsible for the conduct of operations at sea. This report, based on all available intelligence, had shown the nature of the barriers in great detail, including the position of the blockships and any possible gaps in the defences. Lt Cdr Wellner from the *U-16* had recently returned from the area and his reconnaissance on current conditions, radio beacons and guards became the deciding factor on whether to mount another operation. It was decided to give one of the younger and more daring submarine captains the opportunity to try and penetrate the base once more.

The captain in question was Lieutenant Günther Prien who commanded the *U-47*. This submarine had already seen action and was responsible for the sinking of the *Bosnia*; the *Claro* and the *Gartavon* on 5, 6 and 7 September. Prien recounts his first orders to visit the F.d.U. (Führer der U-Boote = Commanding Officer of all submarines).

Meeting place: On board the *Weichsel* at Tirpitz Quay.

In the middle of the room there was a huge table, Commander Sobe, Lt Cdr Wellner and Captain von Friedeburg stood behind it and facing me was the F.d.U. Commodore Dönitz. He shakes my hand and says 'Now listen: Wellner, start again right from the beginning.'

Wellner walks to the table and bows over the chart. 'The guarding is as usual. The special arrangements, which I mentioned in the war diary, are to be found at the following places' (pointing to some spots on the chart).

My eyes follow his hand. He is pointing at the Orkney Islands. In the centre of the chart 'Bay of Scapa Flow' is written in big letters. Wellner continues his explanations, but I can't follow him at the moment. All my thoughts circle around the name: Scapa Flow.

The Commodore tapped the chart with his dividers, 'and here is where the British barriers were during the World War and probably they will be there again. This is the place where Emsmann was destroyed, (pointing to Hoxa Sound) and here are the usual anchorage grounds of the British Navy. All seven entrances to the bay will be blocked and well guarded. In spite of this I could imagine that a determined commanding officer could enter here (pointing to Kirk Sound). It will not be easy, because the current is very strong here between the islands. In spite of this I think it should be possible at the turn of the tide without further ceremony!'

He raised his head. A keen searching eye under a lowered brow.

'What do you think about it Prien ?'

Prien was given forty-eight hours to think the situation over, study the charts and weigh up the consequences of the action he was about to undertake. Prien's thoughts must have cast back to the First World War with the loss of Von Hennig, Hansen and Emsmann when they perished in Hoxa Sound in the *UB-116*.

The very next day he was back in front of the F.d.U.

When I enter, the Great Lion (nick name for Dönitz) is sitting at his desk.

'I report as ordered, Sir'.

He doesn't respond. It seems he missed my military salute.

He only views me with a long look and asks: 'Yes or No ?'

'Yes, Commodore.'

The shadow of a smile. Serious again, he asks insistently: 'Did you think about Emsmann and Hennig?'

'Yes, Sir' I say.
'Then get your boat equipped, you will be told the time of departure'.'

With the outbreak of the Second World War the Orkney Islands and Scapa Flow remained the key to the Royal Navy's North Atlantic strategy. Scapa Flow was considered impenetrable because of the narrow passages between the reefs and islands. Likely attack would be expected only from the skies. Further measures were taken to block the entrances into Scapa Flow by the use of block-ships, mines, anti-submarine nets and barrage of various types.

All of the German intelligence pointed to the chance that a U-boat, under cover of darkness on an incoming high tide, could possibly enter Scapa Flow through Kirk Sound. This passageway had fierce currents, but had still not been completely blocked by the block-ships favoured by the navy at this time. Penetration by the enemy was not considered very easy. Günther Prien was to prove how inadequate the British defences were and made one of the most controversial attacks ever recorded in the annals of naval history.

The Sinking of HMS *Royal Oak*

On the night of 14 October 1939 the battleship HMS *Royal Oak* took up her station at the north east of Scapa Flow in the Orkney Islands at 7.05 p.m. Her duties were to protect the remaining British Fleet, Kirkwall and the RDF (later radar) station at Netherbutton in case of aerial attack. Just twenty years earlier the German Imperial Fleet was interred in this same bay and then scuttled by order of Admiral von Reuter. Near to the *Royal Oak* was an old aircraft carrier, the *Pegasus,* and at the opposite end of the bay near Lyness was the *Iron Duke,* the fleet's flag ship, with three of her original five funnels removed. She was similar in shape to the *Repulse.*

Earlier on the morning of Friday 13 October 1939, the remainder of the British High Seas Fleet had been ordered out of Scapa Flow by Admiral Forbes due to the increasing danger from Luftwaffe reconnaissance flights and the 'bottleneck' that might happen in Scapa Flow should there be a major aerial attack. The fleet sailed for the west coast of Scotland and left the much slower *Royal Oak* to guard the 'station'.

The *Royal Oak* was left in Scapa Flow, as she had recently been fitted with huge anti-submarine attack blisters along the entire length of her hull, these further reduced her manoeuvrability and her speed to only 14 knots. She had also suffered from engine troubles after a severe battering out on patrol in the North Sea and it was feared that she would not be able to keep up with the rest of the fleet when they sailed out to Loch Ewe on the Scottish west coast.

U-boat Commander Prien's latest aerial reports still showed several major British warships at anchor. He decided to press on and entered Scapa Flow

The Orkney Islands, although famous for the sinking of the German Fleet, is equally well known for the sinking of HMS Royal Oak *by a German U-boat. The* Royal Oak *is seen here in the Mediterranean shortly after she had new anti-submarine blisters attached to her hull. It was this extra weight which dictated that she stayed in Scapa Flow while the rest of the Home Fleet sailed to the west coast of Scotland on that fateful day in 1939.*

A calm and peaceful Scapa Bay with HMS Royal Oak *in the foreground resting over the area where the German Fleet sank. Very soon the* Royal Oak, *with 833 dead, would be sunk to the bottom of the bay.*

The Royal Oak *was built in the Naval dockyards at Devonport in Plymouth and was commissioned in May 1916 at a cost of £2.5 million. At over 189.10m long, 31.8m wide and with a hull of 10.10m depth, the* Royal Oak *was also equipped with the largest array of guns ever fitted to a British battleship. These 15in (384mm) guns set in four pairs, were capable of firing one ton (1000 kg) shells over 21km. The* Royal Oak *needed 1,198 men to keep her at battle stations. One of five Royal Sovereign class of battleships, she displaced 29,150 tons and was capable of speeds in excess of twenty-two knots driven by 40,000 horsepower oil-fuelled Parsons turbines. The* Royal Oak *first saw action at the Battle of Jutland and was credited with two hits.*

with surprisingly little difficulty not long after midnight. Kirk Sound was both narrow and shallow and was further hampered by the old and derelict ships sunk deliberately to try and block this entrance into Scapa Flow. No one could have dreamed that Günther Prien would have dared to take such a hazardous route, or imagined that any such mission would be successful.

Finding no immediate danger, or any of the warships in the bay, the *U-47* made a quick cruise around the immediate area and were preparing to leave once more to avoid detection when it spotted HMS *Royal Oak* lying to the north, almost a mile offshore, and what they took to be HMS *Repulse* lying behind her.

Prien's first torpedo supposedly hit the bows of what he thought was the *Repulse*. His second salvo of two torpedoes at 1 a.m. hit the closer target, but inflicted only minor damage, confusing the crew of the *Royal Oak* into thinking that the muffled explosions were an onboard problem, possibly a small explosion in the forward paint store. This gave Commander Prien an additional twenty minutes in which to return to his firing position, reload and fire a second salvo which gave three direct hits amidships and sent the *Royal*

Oak to the seabed in under ten minutes, taking 833 officers and men with her to the bottom.

One of the last men to escape from the *Royal Oak* was Leading Telegraphist Raymond Jones. His watch had stopped at 1.29 a.m. when he jumped into the sea from the upturned, barnacle-laden hull. He was one of the few survivors to be picked up from the ship's carley life rafts, as most of the others were wrecked in their recent foray into the North Sea during a violent storm.

The following dramatic, even dramatized, extract is from the Log of the *U-47*:

Time	Position, Wind etc.	Incidents

14/10/39

0027	It is a very eerie sight. On land everything is dark, high in the sky are the flickering Northern Lights, so that the bay surrounded by highish mountains, is directly lit up from above. The blockships lie in thesound, ghostly as the wings of a theatre.	It is disgustingly light. The whole bay is lit up. To the south of Cava, there is nothing. I go further in. To port I recognise Hoxa Sound Coast guard, to which in the next few minutes the boat must present itself as a target. In that event all would be lost; at present south of Cava no ships are to be seen, although visibility is extremely good. Hence decision.
0055		South of Cava there is no shipping; so before staking everything on success, all possible precautions must be taken. Therefore, turn to port is made. We proceed north by the coast. Two battleships are lying at anchor, and further inshore, destroyers. Cruisers not visible, therefore attack on the big. Distance apart, 3,000 metres.
0116 (time queried in pencil, 0058 suggested)		Estimated depth, 7.5 metres. Impact firing. One torpedo fixed on the northern ship, two on the southern. After a good 3.5 minutes, a torpedo detonates on the northern ship; of the other two
0121 (queried to 0102) suggested time 0123), in pencil		nothing is to be seen. About! Torpedo fired stern; in the bow, two tubes loaded; three torpedoes from the bow. After three tense minutes comes the detonation of the nearer ship. There is a loud explosion, roar and rumbling. Then comes column of water, followed by columns of fire, and splinters fly through the air. I decide to withdraw.

This rather fictionalized account has enraged those men who managed to survive the carnage of that night, furthermore, claims were made that the *U-47* could have been nowhere near Scapa Flow from the logbook description. However, it is assumed that the log was rewritten for the German press to add valour to a rather vainglorious deed.

A more honest version appears in Günther Prien's memoirs:

> I can't take my eyes off the binoculars. It feels like the door to hell has suddenly been wrenched open and I could see straight down into the blazing inferno. I look down into my boat. It is dim and quiet down there...and like never before, I feel an affection to the men down there, who do their duty, silent and blind, who can't see the day or the target they are fighting against and who, if it has to be, will also die in the darkness of our boat.

What was certain was that the strike was so swift and undetected that no one had any inclination of a U-boat attack. There was no search made until long after the *U-47* had escaped from Scapa Flow on an outgoing tide. It was not until the next morning that all available ships made a thorough search of Scapa Flow, dropping depth charges.

The *U-47* had quickly made her escape from Scapa Flow and managed to avoid detection. On returning to her home base at Wilhelmshaven on 17 October, they were met by the Admiral of the Fleet Erich Raeder and Commodore Dönitz and were given a hero's welcome. Prien's submarine used to have a drawing of a skull and crossbones on the conning tower; when she returned to Wilhelmshaven the *U-47* had a snorting bull newly-painted by her crew. Henceforth she was known as 'The Bull Of Scapa Flow'. Lieutenant Commander Prien and his crew were flown on Hitler's private aeroplane to Templehof Airport in Berlin and escorted to the Reichskanzlei (the Chancellery) to an audience with the Führer. Prien was awarded the Ritterkreuz des Eisemen Kreuzes (Knight's Cross of the Iron Cross) First Class by Hitler.

Prien's crew had been credited with a hit on the *Repulse* by Dönitz, but the Royal Navy still vehemently deny that she was even in Scapa Flow. Prien never actually confirmed that he had hit the *Repulse*, but the media circus was already well underway and the new heroes of Germany never got the chance to deny the claim either. If a second ship had been hit, it is now assumed that the second ship may have been the *Iron Duke*, which for some reason had travelled up to that end of Scapa Flow for additional protection. The *Iron Duke* was actually very similar in shape to the *Repulse*, as three of her five funnels had been removed. At night and in low light against the hills in the background, her silhouette would have indeed been very similar to the *Repulse*. Somehow the *Iron Duke* had been holed and it is thought that she managed to limp back to Lyness where she was beached to await repairs. It was during these repairs that she was bombed by four Junkers-88 of the 1/K.G.30

While the loss of the Royal Oak *was still reverberating around the British Isles, Günther Prien and the crew of* the U-47 *had returned to her home base where they were greeted as heroes. The conning tower of the submarine had been repainted with a snorting bull. From that day onward, Prien and his ship were known as the 'Bull of Scapa Flow'. The U-47 displaced 857 tons submerged, had five torpedo tubes, and had a compliment of fifteen torpedos or fourteen mines, as well as two smaller deck mounted guns. Capable of speeds in excess of seventeen knots on the surface, but only eight knots submerged she was 65m long (218ft).*

A rare photograph taken of Prien and his crew by an unknown photographer. Ranged over the conning tower, the crew of forty-four were treated as heroes. Prien and his officers were flown to Berlin to be presented to Adolf Hitler who awarded them the Iron Cross.

More pictures of Günther Prien, the U-boat captain whose sinking of the Royal Oak won him high acclaim in Nazi Germany.

ADMIRAL JELLICOE'S FLAGSHIP
H.M.S. "IRON DUKE"
(LEADING BATTLE FLEET TO SEA)

It was Admiral Jellico's Flagship, the Iron Duke *which was also at station in Scapa Flow the night HMS* Royal Oak *was sunk. It was thought that the* Iron Duke *was hit on the same night as the* Royal Oak, *as it is confused with the* Repulse. *The U-boat stated that it hit the* Repulse.

group three days later on 17 October. The news of the possible hit on the *Iron Duke / Repulse* has always been denied to try and lessen the impact of the raid and the subsequent loss of morale.

The attack on the *Royal Oak* was so sudden and so catastrophic that there was little chance for the crew who were still, for the most part, in their beds. Cordite and explosives ignited almost immediately and the ship rapidly took in water. Her main armaments had not been locked in position, nor were her hatches secured. The weight of the big guns pulled the ship over onto her starboard side and water flooded in through the open hatches. Survivors tell of the ignition of the cordite in the magazine which was like 'facing a giant blowtorch, it set fire to hammocks, fittings and men, it peeled the skin off their faces and arms like paper off a wall'. Corporal N.T. (Taff) Davies was asleep in the Corporal's Locker, just forward of the R.M. Mess deck on the starboard side. After the first explosion he climbed up a ladder into the admiral's galley flat, then out onto the quarter-deck. He could not believe what had happened. First thoughts were that they had hit a mine, or that there had been an aerial strike. However, when the next three explosions occurred and the ship heeled over onto its side he realized that it had been attacked by submarine.

Throughout the early hours of that terrible morning, the Fraserburgh-registered steam drifter *Daisy II* kept going back to the scene of the disaster.

These rare postcard-format photographs taken on board the Royal Oak by members of the crew recently came up at auction from a private collector. They give a rare insight into the lives of the men. The fore deck was a mass of massive anchor chains, running from the capstans to the anchor lockers. Each link was over 30cm long (12in) and

are now hanging vertically from the upturned Royal Oak *dropping to the seabed. Her second gun emplacement in front of the main bridge also held a small biplane launcher, seen here quite clearly in the photograph. Various groups of lads would have their photograph taken to send home to sweethearts and family.*

The *Daisy II* had actually been moored along the port side of the *Royal Oak* when she was torpedoed and was almost pulled underwater by her mooring lines when the *Oak* healed over to starboard. The quick thinking by crewman Johnnie Duthie, who cut the lines with an axe, saved the ship for the heartbreaking task which lay ahead of them. The crew, skippered by John Gatt, battled throughout the night to pluck wounded, burned and exhausted sailors from the sea. In all, the six man crew on their tiny steam drifter rescued 360 men on that fateful night, John Gatt later received the DSC for his services.

Survivors and bodies were taken to the *Pegasus* all night long. One eyewitness on the ship said '*Pegasus* was in a shambles with oily bodies, which we took as many as possible to the engine room to thaw out, making large amounts of hot cocoa and tea and mustering all available clothing for the survivors to wear. Several bodies which were beyond help were placed outside the sick bay on *Pegasus*. Later that day we moved billets to other end of Scapa Flow near HMS *Iron Duke*. Air Raid warning but no action. Survivors were then taken aboard *Voltaire*'.

The Royal Oak *was a formidable fighting ship, but was getting rather long in the tooth for active duty in the Atlantic Fleet due to her slower speed compared with the new design of* Revenge-*class battleships. Her anti-submarine blisters further slowed her down and so it was decided to leave her on active duty in northern Scapa Flow as likely attack of Kirkwall was expected to come by air. Sadly, this miscalculation, as well as a number of other fatal mistakes, led to the loss of the ship and 833 of her officers and men on the night of 13 October 1939.*

A formal photograph of the crew of the Royal Oak, two-thirds of whom would not survive the attack by the U-47.

The following signal was received by the *Pegasus* from Captain Benn.

> From: Captain Benn (*Royal Oak*) on *Voltaire*
> To: HMS *Pegasus*
> Officers and men of the *Royal Oak*, whom you assisted so
> magnificently last night, can never express, and never forget the
> debt of gratitude which they owe to you all.

In all, there were 414 survivors, but many were very badly burned from cordite and fuel oil and many more perished from prolonged exposure in those cold, northern waters. The death toll mounted in the years that followed due to the problems suffered by the inhalation and swallowing of fuel oil. The first of the funerals was held at the Naval Cemetery at Lyness on the Island of Hoy directly behind the Fleet Headquarters. Twenty-four men were buried on 16 October amid further air raid warnings, attended by survivors.

Ironically, that same weekend, after the sinking of the *Royal Oak*, the last derelict ship arrived in Scapa Flow and was sunk in Kirk Sound, effectively blocking all other passage through the Sound. Soon after, Winston Churchill, on visiting the scene, ordered the complete blockage of all the sounds to the east of Scapa Flow. Four barriers were to be built in all, with the 'help' of Italian Prisoners of War. These are still known to this day as the Churchill Barriers.

While escorting a North Atlantic convoy on 8 March 1941, the *Wolverine* sighted the *U-47* on the surface and engaged her in action. With her

Survivors and other ships' crews follow in procession to the Naval cemetery behind Lyness naval base on the Island of Hoy on 16 October 1939. Such was the tragic loss just six weeks into the start of the Second World War, that the British Admiralty was in disarray. Sir Winston Churchill immediately travelled up to the Orkney Islands and the construction of the now famous Churchill Barriers was begun.

distinctive snorting bull on the conning tower, the crew of the *Wolverine* were keen to avenge the loss of the *Royal Oak* and kept up a continuous bombardment until they became dangerously low on both fuel and ammunition. The *U-47* was lost with all forty-eight hands that same day, including eight who had been in Scapa Flow: Prien, Biermann, Bohm, Hotzer, Sammann, Steinhagen, Thewes and Werder.

Underwater on HMS *Royal Oak*

HMS *Royal Oak* now rests on her starboard side, but almost upside down at 135° to the vertical in 29m of water. Her keel, camouflaged by over fifty-five years of marine growth is now encrusted in kelp, soft corals, known as dead man's fingers, and anemones. The upturned hull has the appearance of an underwater cliff and as you descend, more and more of the superstructure is covered in anemones, tube worms, brittle starfish and many varieties of fish, shrimps, crabs and starfish.

When you reach the port railings at 16m and stare down into the gloom, nothing prepares you for that mixture of fear, excitement and raw adrenaline at this depth. There is very little ambient light and you look down into the darkened depths created by the shadow of the upturned hull. Swimming out and away from the hull, to avoid descending into the labyrinth of twisted metal, you finally land on the seabed at 32m. Turning around, you can just make out the silhouette of this massive ship, but as you approach her once more, the visibility deteriorates rapidly as the rust particles and other debris now hang like a permanent shroud around the ship.

The eerieness increases the closer you approach the upturned ship, the atmosphere is almost palpable as you swim under the hull to inspect the guns and other more recognizable parts. Accompanied by a Royal Navy diver on oxygen rebreathers that stop the debris from landing on our heads, which would have been knocked off by conventional exhausted air bubbles and also to allow safer bottom time at these depths, we examined areas of the superstructure, companionways and hatches. Everywhere there was clear evidence of the ship's deterioration and collapsing metal plates. Many steel plates had 'sprung', some of them stretching over 10m to the seabed and there was a very real danger that our equipment and surface lines could become snagged on the superstructure.

Coming back out into safer waters, we were able to explore those sections of the hull, mastheads and conning tower which were ripped off when this massive ship hit the seabed. The spotting top, which was once 28m above the waves, now lies crumpled and rusting on the seabed. The admiral's steam pinnace, which was dragged under when the *Royal Oak* sunk, now rests vertically, but is collapsing onto her port side. This small 8m support craft is an eerie sight, but she is dwarfed by the massive superstructure looming overhead.

The admiral's barge where it reests on the sea bed near the remains of the Royal Oak.

The breaches of the 15in guns are over 3m across and you can almost swim into the barrels which are still embedded in the sea floor and actually support the larger part of the ship. Open hatches and companionways are testimony to the rapid sinking of the ship and the links of her anchor chain, each over 1ft long, drop to the sea bed. Anti-aircraft guns still have their ammunition intact in their racks and the smaller 6in and 4in guns stretch out into the Orkney waters, completely covered in a mantle of plumose anemones, sponges and starfish. Evidence of the attack can be found in the crumpled bows of the ship and from the massive hole amidships where the twisted sheets of metal plate edge a hole over 8m across. Scallops, seapens, mussels and crabs can be found on the seabed amidst ammunition and the debris from over fifty-five years of underwater deterioration.

At one time, there was a rumour that the ship had been sunk by saboteurs with an explosive charge in the engine room. Examination of the hull shows no evidence of an internal explosion. The buckled plates are pushed inwards and remains of the torpedo firing mechanism were found and identified by local divers.

The hull comes to within 5m of the surface and it is here that the Royal Navy Clearance Diving Team make their annual pilgrimage to unfold the battle ensign and once more fly this flag from the stern of the *Royal Oak* in memory of those 833 men who lost their lives. The battle ensign is attached to the port propeller shaft which is now located in a depth of 15m. Her propellers were removed many years ago.

As the hull deteriorates and the internal seams crack and split open, the light fuel oil has found its way out through the hull. Even after all this time, the seepage of oil is clearly visible as it makes its way to the surface as tiny globules, almost 'smartie shaped'. On the surface, the oil rapidly spreads into a rainbow coloured film which stretches for hundreds of metres across the waters of Scapa Flow. There are plans to remove the remaining oil, under increasing environmental pressure, but the local Orcadians would prefer the oil to stay on board and continue to leak as a permanent reminder of the ships' last position. As an interim move an effort has been made to aid the clean up, with the erection of a large container over the worst affected area. This collects the escaping oil, which is then pumped into a support craft.

The location of the stricken *Royal Oak* is near to a large, green channel buoy, although this is not necessary due to the issue of fuel oil to the surface, it serves as a poignant reminder to the dramatic events which happened on the night of 14 October 1939. On the buoy is a plaque which reads

THIS MARKS THE WRECK OF HMS *ROYAL OAK*
AND THE GRAVE OF HER CREW.
RESPECT THEIR RESTING PLACE.
UNAUTHORISED DIVING PROHIBITED.

The *Royal Oak* is one of the most intact sunken battleships in the world and ranks as the top shipwreck in European waters and one of the top six in the world. The *Royal Oak* is a designated war grave and is protected by Navy Law. Diving on her is strictly forbidden, and it is only on the anniversary of her sinking that a team of Navy divers is allowed to descend through these chilly waters which conceal her watery grave.

The author, Lawson Wood, was granted a special dispensation by the Ministry of Defence to accompany the dive team on the anniversary of her sinking and was in fact responsible for discovering the exact area on the ship's hull where the oil was leaking through. He has had many hours recorded diving on this grand ship, and his unique set of underwater photographs that document her position and inevitable destruction are included in this book.

The only dive team in the world allowed to dive this historic wreck is The Northern Diving Unit, now stationed at Faslane Royal Navy Base on the Clyde. Each year this highly trained, specialist clearance diving unit make their annual pilgrimage to the Orkney Islands to inspect and survey the inevitable deterioration of this once proud battleship and to raise the battle ensign once more. Attached to the port propeller shaft, the ensign is made secure for the coming year, the year old ensign is removed from its position and cleaned. This is then presented to the Royal Oak Survivors Association and then passed on to various groups of servicemen and organizations who were represented on the *Royal Oak*.

8

The Barriers

The Blockships

The blockships were a combination of rusting hulks, derelict and captured shipping and decommissioned merchantmen, many bought from ship breakers. They were deliberately sunk or scuttled in the shallower entrances along the eastern approaches to Scapa Flow where the strong tidal race alone was not enough to deter any incursion of enemy shipping. Penetration into Scapa Flow, it was always thought, would come from a submarine and it was deemed that the best and quickest possible way to block the entrances to the eastern approaches was with sunken ships. At least by blocking the four entrances to the east, any other activity would have to be concentrated to the south and west where better systems of defence were being prepared.

Kirk Sound between Orkney Mainland and Lamb Holm had ten ships sunk; Skerry Sound, between Lamb Holm and Glims Holm had twelve blockships, East Weddel Sound between Glims Holm and Burray had five ships and Water Sound between Burray and South Ronaldsay had a further nine blockships. Eight ships were also sunk in Burra Sound to the west. A total 50,000 tons of shipping was sunk in one year alone and over 100,000 tons of shipping sunk in the two wars. It was only after the disastrous loss of HMS *Royal Oak* that Winston Churchill ordered the building of the now famous Churchill Barriers across the same stretches of water which had previously failed to keep out the *U-47*.

Kirk Sound (No.1 Barrier)

Numidian   4,836 ton steamer, built in Glasgow 1891, sunk in 1914, salvaged in 1924.

Thames   1,327 ton steamer, built in Glasgow 1887, sunk in 1914.

Aoarangi	4,268 ton steamer, built in Glasgow 1883, sunk in 1914.
Busk	367 ton steamer, built in North Shields 1906, sunk in 1940.
Gambhira	5,257 ton steamer, built in Sunderland 1910, sunk in 1939, salvaged in 1943, used as ASDIC target and sunk again off N. Wales.
Lake Neuchatel	3,859 ton steamer, built in Sunderland 1907, sunk in 1939, salvaged in 1948.
Minieh	2,890 ton steamer, built in Glasgow, sunk in 1915, hull salvaged.
Redstone	3,110 ton steamer, built in West Hartlepool 1918, sunk in 1940, salvaged.
Seriano	3,543 ton steamer, built in Michigan, sunk in 1939, salvaged.
Tabarka	2,624 ton steamer, built in Rotterdam 1909, seized in 1940, sunk in Kirk Sound in 1941, refloated in 1944 and sunk again in Burra Sound.

Skerry Sound (No.2 Barrier)

Rosewood	1,757 ton steamer built in South Shields 1889, sunk in 1915.
Teeswood	1,589 ton steamer, built in 1882, sunk in 1914.
Lycia	2,338 ton motorship, built in Port Glasgow 1924, sunk in 1940.
Ilenstein	1,508 ton steamer, built in Kiel 1898, sunk in 1940.
Cape Ortegal	4,896 ton steamer, built in Glasgow 1911, sunk in 1939.
Elton	2,461 ton steamer, built in West Hartlepool 1880, sunk in 1915.
Emerald Wings	2,139 ton steamer, built in Cherbourg 1920, sunk in 1940
Rheinfeld	3,634 ton steamer, built in Newcastle 1893, sunk in 1914.
F/C Pontoon	A crane barge used by Metal Industries, sunk in 1941.
Almeria	2,418 ton steamer, built in Sunderland, sunk in 1915.
Argyle	1185 ton steamer, built in Hull, sunk in 1914
A.C.6.	Metal Industries barge, sunk in 1941.

East Weddel Sound (No.3 Barrier)

Lapland	1,234 ton steamer, built in Dundee 1890, sunk in 1915.
Reginald	930 ton schooner, built in Glasgow 1878, sunk in 1915.
Empire Seaman	1,921 ton steamer, built in Lubeck, seized and sunk in 1940.
Gartshore	1,564 ton steamer, built in South Shields 1880, sunk in 1915, no trace left.
Martis	2,483 ton steamer, built in South Shields 1894, sunk in 1940.

At Barrier No.2 across Skerry Sound, between Lamb Holm and Glimps Holm, three blockships were placed in position, the Lycia, Ilsenstein *and* Emerald Wings *were set to reduce the initial flow of the tide. Gradually, the sound was filled by dropping concrete blocks and rough hewn stone from the nearby quarries from a cable car strung across the sound.*

Another view of Barrier No.2 at Skerrie Sound. In the distance you can see the progress being made on Barrier No.3 across Weddell Sound between Glimps Holm and Burray.

Water Sound (No.4 Barrier)

Carron	1,017 ton steamer, built in Dundee 1894, sunk in 1940.
Collingdoc	1,780 ton steamer, built in 1925, Ontario, Canada 1925, sunk in 1942.
Lorne	1,186 ton steamer, built in Hull 1873, sunk in 1915.
Gondolier	173 ton paddle steamer, built in Glasgow 1866, sunk in 1940.
Carolina Thorden	3,645 ton tanker, built in Sweden, bombed off Faroes, sunk in 1942.
Juanita	1139 ton motor tanker built in Sunderland 1918, sunk in 1940.
Pontos	2,265 ton steamer, built in Glasgow 1891, sunk in 1914.
Clio	2,733 ton steamer, built in Hartlepool 1889, sunk in 1914.
Naja	Concrete Barge sunk in 1939.

Burra Sound

Inverlane	8,900 ton tanker, built in Vegesack, Germany, stern removed attached to another ship and then mined off South Shields in 1939, bow sunk in 1944.
Gobernador Bories	2,332 ton steamer, built in West Hartlepool 1882, sunk in 1915.

Tabarka	2,624 ton steamer, built in Rotterdam 1909, seized in 1940, sunk in Kirk Sound in 1941, refloated in 1944 and sunk again in Burra Sound.
Doyle	1,761 ton steamer, built in Troon, sunk in 1940.
Budrie	2,252 ton steamer, built in Glasgow 1882, sunk in 1915.
Rotherfield	2,831 ton steamer, built in West Hartlepool 1889, sunk in 1914, blown up and dispersed in 1962.
Ronda	1,941 ton steamer, built in Sunderland, sunk in 1915, blown up and dispersed in 1962.
Urmstone Grange	3,423 ton steamer, built in Belfast 1894, sunk in 1914, blown up and dispersed in 1962.

Diving the Blockships

Now, more than eighty years after the sinking of many of the ships, the wrecks are still making history, as one of the greatest dive attractions in Europe. Conditions vary tremendously during the season. The visibility is generally poor and dark on the seabed in the centre of Scapa Flow, lights should always be used and work-up dives should be undertaken before you do the deeper battleships. That is why so many photographers prefer the block ships at the entrance to Burra Sound, where the average depth is half that of the German warships, giving them much more light, more interesting marine growth and much clearer water, as the tidal race at Burra Sound sweeps all sedimentation particles away. However, this also means that you have only limited time on these wrecks and then only at slack tide. The Burra Sound wrecks are the most photogenic although there is not as much mystique attached to them as to the scuttled German fleet.

Much of the wreckage from the ships now lying alongside the Churchill Barriers is well broken up and is scattered over a wide area. The average depth of the sound is around 8m (27ft) deep, but it does reach as far as 15m (50ft) in Kirk Sound. The larger wrecks are still evident on the eastern side of the barriers, the most obvious are the *Pontos, Caron* and *Collingdoc* at Barrier 4; the distinctive *Elton* at Barrier 2; and the stern of the *Reginald* at Barrier 3. Most divers tend to dive on the more sheltered, western side of the barriers and visit ships such as the *Numidian* at Barrier 1 and the *Empire Seaman* at Barrier 3. The only visible blockship in Burra Sound to the west used to be that of the *Inverlane*. Until a few years ago, the wreckage of this ship was perhaps the most distinctive of all the wrecks, with her bows and foremast rising clear of Burra Sound. Sadly, the ship has finally collapsed in on itself and rolled over under the continuous onslaught of the strong currents which sweep four times daily, in and out of Scapa Flow.

The best blockships for diving are undoubtedly those in Burra Sound but, due to the massive movement of water, you are only ever able to dive the three main wrecks at slack water. All of the Scapa Flow dive-boat skippers are very experienced in these waters and their advice should always be sought before entering the water.

Sadly, the *Inverlane* is no longer a safe, viable dive, she was once perhaps the best dive in Scapa Flow. At one time, dive-boat captains moored alongside the stricken ship and you actually climbed onto the hulk and dived inside her cavernous interior. The ship is still available for those who know the site. The *Tabarka* lies upside down, her empty hull is a refuge for divers and is covered in marine life. The *Doyle* and *Gobernador Bories* are perhaps the most photogenic of all and certainly have the most marine life. Lying in 15m (50ft) of water, they are largely intact and perfect for penetration and photography.

The most popular is the *Gobernador Bories*, formerly known as the *Wordsworth* and weighed 2,332 tons. She was an iron single-screw steamer, built in 1882 at West Hartlepool and registered in Punta Arenas in Chile. The *Gobernador Bories* was sunk in 1915 and is considered to be the most popular of the blockships with divers, as her sinking dates from around the same period as the internment of the German Fleet. Now lying in 16m of water, the hull is fairly well broken up and angled over to port. The main, wooden decking has all gone now, leaving the metal spars all covered in kelp, soft corals, pin cushion starfish and hydroids. The bow and stern are almost completely intact and her propeller is still visible. The underside of the bow is completely covered in plumose anemones (*Metridium senile*). Due to the open aspect of the wreck, there is quite a lot of shelter from the current and divers are able to enter the main part of the forward section through two fairly open areas amid the tangled wreckage. The inside of the hull is quite open and uncluttered, except for the families of ballan wrasse which follow you into the ship. The upright spars near the stern have pincushion starfish, hydroids, small seasquirts and red and brown algae. This dive should only be undertaken at slack water and then only on advice from the dive boat skipper.

Smaller amounts of wreckage are found on the sites of the former *Rotherfield, Urmstone Grange, Ronda* and *Budrie*. The blockships located to the east, lying alongside the Churchill Barriers, are used for training dives and for easy exploration and photography. These ships are all topped with kelp and their open decking spars are now covered in small anemones, sea urchins and starfish and are surrounded by resident groups of ballan wrasse.

Near the *Gobernador Baries* is the *Doyle*, a single-screw steamer built in Troon and registered in Belfast, that displaced 1,761 tons. The *Doyle* joined her sister blockships at Burra Sound in 1940. Similar in profile to the *Gobernador Bories*, the *Doyle* lies in 16m of water (54ft). Fairly intact, the ship sits upright with a steep list to port, her huge rudder and propeller are still intact. Quite open for exploration, the wreck is topped with kelp, surrounded by schools of fish and is smothered in invertebrate marine life from anemones to sea slugs, all vying for space on the old, steel ribs and hull.

The Churchill Barriers

The eastern approaches to Scapa Flow were thought to be impregnable to enemy shipping with its combination of narrow channels, blockships and fierce currents. The dreadful shock and distress caused by the sinking of HMS *Royal Oak* was to shake the naval establishment to its decks, just six weeks after war between Britain and Germany was declared.

In a reprisal attack on the naval fortress of Scapa Flow for the sinking of the *UB116*, the *U47*, commanded by Gunther Prien, performed an incredible feat of maritime daring when it was stealthily manoeuvred into Scapa Flow and back out to safety after sinking HMS *Royal Oak* in the early hours of 14 October 1939. 833 officers and men lost their lives that night, the nation was stunned into action and the First Lord of the Admiralty, Winston Churchill travelled to Orkney to see what could be done to safeguard Scapa Flow and her fleet from any future enemy attack.

Great barriers were to be built in place of the blockships and Sir Arthur Whitaker, Civil Engineer-in-Chief to the Admiralty surveyed the sites aboard his survey vessel HMS *Franklin*. A scale model was quickly built at Manchester University and Balfour Beatty were appointed the contractors for this massive task. Not only were the tidal races to be stemmed, a road was also to be built on the barriers to link the south-eastern Orkney Islands.

Work started on 10 May 1940 when the 15,551 ton liner SS *Almanzora* arrived off Holm carrying all the necessary equipment to start the construction site, including a couple of Thames barges, the *Roman* and the *Gatville*. Moss Quarry on Holm was considered by the engineers to be the best site for the infill and that is just what they set out to do 'fillin in the sea' it was called at the time. New piers were built on each of the islands to facilitate the shifting of massive blocks of stone from the quarries as well as for the construction camps. Much of the rock was moved by Bedford truck and local railway line with side tipping trucks wherever possible. However, as the war progressed in the south, more men from the Balfour Beatty work force were called up. Coupled with the adverse working conditions, the work schedule began to slow down over the second winter on Orkney. Paid holidays were introduced for the first time ever to try and persuade locals to work, but still the work on the barriers fell behind schedule. What was to be done?

During the African Campaign, thousands of Italian soldiers were captured and interred in Britain. It was agreed that this 'special work force' would make suitable conscripts for the work of building the barriers. Six hundred prisoners of war were marshalled at Edinburgh's Waverley Station under the command of Major J.C. Yates, from there they transferred to Aberdeen docks where they boarded a boat for Orkney in January 1942. This number would quickly rise to over 1,000 prisoners of war. Conditions were harsh for the Italians, with hard work or forced labour as well as having to contend with the biting cold of the Orkney winters. Gradually they proved themselves to be able workmen and

Huge concrete blocks were constructed by Italian prisoners of war drafted into the work by Winston Churchill. They quickly proved themselves able workers and were quite often left unattended in charge of the machinery. Weighing four to five tons apiece, these concrete blocks are carried by small railway line and then hoisted onto the cableway, known as 'blondins' and drawn across the various sounds by a pulley system and dropped in strategic positions. Several of the old moulds for the blocks can still be seen at the barriers.

Just after construction, you can quite clearly see the method of placing blocks of varying sizes in appropriate positions to strengthen the causeway and provide a stable foundation for the road. The first barrier was completed across Kirk Sound by August 1943. It was through Kirk Sound that the U-47 had made entry and exit after the successful attack on HMS Royal Oak.

indeed helped tremendously. Many were given jobs with more authority and a mutual respect rose between the prisoners and guards.

Gradually the barriers were extended between the islands, creating dramatic waterfalls and rapids as the rising and falling tide continued to beat against these new defences. Huge cableways spanned the islands, known as 'blondins', these cables were of $2\frac{1}{2}$ in diameter, controlled by winchmen who handled the 'travellers' or carts which dumped rock spill. Over this infill, which was dumped from the cableway and rail, five ton concrete blocks were dropped down each ridge of the 'bolster dams'. As they broke surface, ten ton blocks were positioned by hand and dropped into position to stem the flow of the sea. Once this had been attained, further 4.8 ton blocks were used to form the base of the new roadway which ran the length of the barriers. For the first time, the islands of Lambholm, Glimsholm and Burray were connected to the Orkney mainland in the north to South Ronaldsay in the south. A number of the old bolsters, or concrete moulds, are still to be seen at the edge of causeway, these moulds actually formed 66,000 concrete blocks and spanned three stretches of water, which has a maximum depth of 18m (60ft) in Kirk Sound. (It was through Kirk Sound that the *U-47* gained entry into Scapa Flow).

By August 1943, the first barrier across Kirk Sound was complete enough for escorting troops and Italian prisoners to leave Lambholm to work in the quarry. The newly-opened Strond Cinema in Holm was a godsend and local entrepreneur John Marwick was soon showing films to a wide and varied audience, including the Italians. Almost simultaneously, the shortest stretch at

WATER SOUND CAUSEWAY, CHURCHILL BARRIERS, CONNECTING BURRAY AND SOUTH RONALDSAY

The barrier causeway at Water Sound, with its road along the top.

Another view of a barrier road in Orkney.

1,400ft across Burray Sound at Barrier No.3 was completed using five-ton blocks, as the depth was much less and the current not as strong. It was the Italians who gained full credit for this feat. No longer regarded as prisoners of war, or even the 'enemy', these men were accepted openly on the islands and great pride was taken in their work.

By September 1944, the barriers were all but complete and the majority of the Italians left Orkney. A few stayed behind to assist Domenico Chiocchetti to complete the work on the chapel. The Italians had not only proved themselves able workers, many were now great friends of the islanders and it was with some sadness when most of the work force eventually left and returned to their homeland. Not only had they built great barriers to prevent enemy shipping from ever again entering Scapa Flow from the eastern approaches, they changed the lives of the residents on the southern islands forever, by providing the means of a safe road link to the Orkney mainland, foregoing the necessity for travelling by boat.

The Italian Chapel

Many of those interred were craftsmen who made souvenirs to sell on the islands and there were also many fine artists. One such man was Domenico Chiocchetti who constructed a concrete St George and the Dragon to preside over the camp square. His fine workmanship was recognized and he was given

HOLM - ORKNEY MAINLAND

ITALIAN CHAPEL

LAMB HOLM

GLIMPS HOLM

BURRAY

CHURCHILL BARRIERS, SCAPA FLOW - FROM THE AIR

23940

This fine aerial postcard clearly shows three of the barriers and the location of the Italian Chapel on Lamb Holm. The construction of the barriers has completely altered the tidal flow of the eastern seaboard of the Orkneys and for the first time linked the southern islands to the mainland.

permission to transform a Nissen hut on Lambholm into a chapel. Originally meant to be a school with a chapel at one end, the whole hut became a chapel. Painting was done by Chiocchetti, the wrought iron work by Palumbo and the electrical work by Micheloni.

It is now known as The Italian Chapel. The painting inside is exquisite; hand moulded concrete work enhances the altar and stoop, two of the windows were painted to resemble stained glass and the centrepiece of the Madonna and Child was painted by Chiocchetti. The facade of the hut was transformed by concrete gothic pillars and a belfry. Now a place of pilgrimage by many visitors to the Orkneys, the Italian Chapel and statue of St George are all that remain of the Italian camps.

Built by the Italian Prisoners of War and lovingly painted by Domenico Chiocchetti, the former Nissen hut is a celebration of the Italians' skills during a time of extreme hardship for them.

Bibliography

Gerald Bowman, *The Man Who Bought A Navy* (Harrap)
The Diving Cellar, Stromness, *Divers Guide to the wreck sites in the Orkney Islands*
Johnnie Duthie, *Lest We Forget Daisy*
David M. Ferguson, *Shipwrecks of Orkney, Shetland and Pentland Firth* (David & Charles)
David M. Ferguson, *The Wrecks of Scapa Flow* (Orkney Press)
S.C. George, *Jutland to Junkyard* (Birlinn)
Robert Glenton, *The Royal Oak Affair* (Pen and Sword Books)
The Graphic Newspaper, 1939
W.S. Hewison, *Scapa Flow in War and Peace* (Bellavista Publications)
Imperial Club Magazine, 1940
Alexander Korganoff, *The Phantom of Scapa Flow* (Ian Allan)
James Macdonald, *Churchill's Prisoners* (Orkney Wireless Museum)
Rod Macdonald, *Dive Scapa Flow* (Mainstream Publishing)
Alexander McKee, *Black Saturday* (New English Library)
J. Pottinger, *The Salving of the German Fleet* (Stromness Museum)
P.O.W. Preservation Committee, *Orkney's Italian Chapel*
Günther Prien, *Mein Weg nach Scapa Flow* (Deutscher Verlag 1940)
Peter L. Smith, *The Naval Wrecks of Scapa Flow* (Orkney Press)
Douglas Thomson, *226 Heavy Anti-Aircraft Battery*
Dan Van Der Vat, *The Grand Scuttle* (Birlinn)
Ludwig von Reuter, *Scapa Flow-Das Grab der Deutscher Flotte* (Leipzig, 1921)
H.J. Weaver, *Nightmare at Scapa Flow* (Cressrelles Publishing Co.)
Lawson Wood, *Diving and Snorkelling Guide to Scotland* (Lonely Planet/Pisces Editions)